Great Grandma's Shawl

Great Grandma's Shawl

Diana Levine

To order additional copies of this book, contact:
Xlibris Corporation
1-888-795-4274
www.Xlibris.com
Orders@Xlibris.com
38869

CONTENTS

PART ONE
GREAT GRANDMA'S SHAWL 11
When Great Grandma came to America from Russia in 1912, she
was wearing a shawl she had made for the trip. That shawl is still in the family.

PART TWO
THE BUDD ROAD BUDDIES 21
A group of five girls who are cousins and close friends share many different
adventures.

PART THREE
MA, I DON'T WANNA GO 45
A boy is given a gift of a week in baseball camp, but he doesn't want to go.
He is coaxed into going and at the end of the week he doesn't want to go home.

PART FOUR
DAVIE'S ACCOMPLISHMENT 53
An eight year old boy makes an unassisted triple play in a Little League game.

PART FIVE
A DEER NAMED VELVET 59
A family of four deer lived on the author's lawn one year.

PART SIX
CAT'S IN THE DOG HOUSE 65
A cat and dog become friends.

PART SEVEN
JUDY'S SON 69
is about a biracial couple and the son of the father.
This story has an O. Henry twist!

PART EIGHT
WHAT HAVE WE DONE? 79
This is a tragic but true story told as fiction about a teenager who shot and killed his father so he could have an affair with his stepmother.

PART NINE
MY MOTHER IS ALSO MY MOTHER-IN-LAW 93
A man's widowed mother marries his wife's widowed father.

ACKNOWLEDGEMENT

This book would no be possible without the help and loyalty of Diane Genender who has been my typist

PART ONE

GREAT GRANDMA'S SHAWL

Malka sat in her favorite chair in front of the fireplace working on a big black shawl. It was 1912. Malka was 13 years old. Snow fell heavily outside. There is a lot of snow in White Russia where Malka lived and the large shawl would keep her warm. But Malka was not making it to wear in Russia. She was making it to wear on the trip she and her parents would soon be taking when they would be coming to America.

"Momma," Malka said, "black is too old looking for me, but we have no other wool. What can you do to make it pretty?"

"Let me look through my sewing box," replied her mother. "I think I have some colorful pieces of wool that I can weave through the black."

Malka's mother found some red, yellow, pink, bright blue and white pieces of wool. When Malka finished her knitting, Malka's mother weaved the different pieces of wool into a design of pretty flowers throughout the shawl.

"How's that?" she asked her daughter when she was finished.

"It's beautiful," Malka agreed, giving her mother a hug and kiss. "Thank you, Momma."

"Show it to your father when he comes home," Malka's mother suggested.

As soon as Malka's father came in, Malka grabbed his arm and asked him to sit down. "I have something to show you," she said. Malka put the shawl on and modeled it for him.

"That shawl is beautiful," Malka's father said. "And you are beautiful." Getting up he warmly wrapped his arms around his daughter and kissed her on top of her head.

Over dinner that night Malka's father told Malka and her mother that he had received a letter from Uncle Hershel in New York City telling him that everything was set for them to come. In those days a person neededto have a sponsor before they could come to America.

"Joseph, that's so good," said Malka's mother. "But yet it is so sad. We will be leaving our friends behind."

"Hannah, maybe they will be able to come to America soon, too, and we'll see them in a free land."

"When will we be able to leave?" Malka excitedly asked her father.

"As soon as we pack and get the tickets for the train and the ship."

The next few weeks were spent packing their clothes and saying goodbye to their friends.

On the day they left a neighbor took them to the train station in his horse drawn wagon.

The family boarded the train that was taking them to a seaport where they would board the ship for their long journey across the Atlantic Ocean.

The weather was cold and the wind blew furiously. Malka shivered under her shawl. Her mother who had made a shawl too drew her shawl around her and Malka's father. The three stood closely together. As the ship pulled away from the shore, they cried both from happiness and sadness.

The trip was hard. They slept on mattresses on the floor. The food was poor. And it was cold. But the family stayed together and huddled under the two warm shawls.

One morning Malka's father shook his daughter and wife awake. "Hurry and get dressed," he urged. "There is something I want you to see."

"What's the matter, Joseph?" Malka's mother asked.

"Hannah, just get dressed so we can go up on deck. Malka, quickly now get dressed."

The three hurried up on deck.

"Look," Malka's father said to Malka and her mother, pointing to a statue on an island the ship was nearing. "That's the Statue of Liberty. We're in America."

The three joined the others cheering as the ship slid past the Statue of Liberty and headed to the dock on Ellis Island.

Getting off the ship they were ushered into a large room.

"Look how many people are here" Malka gasped. "What's going to happen here?" She saw people being examined and it scared her. "Poppa," she whispered, "I'm afraid."

"Don't be, my darling. I won't let anyone hurt you."

But when it was their turn to be examined, Malka wouldn't let the doctor touch her. Malka's father held her tight in his strong arms so the doctor could examine her. Still she cried. After Malka's parents were examined, Malka apologized for crying. Her parents told her it was all right to be afraid because this was a new experience. "But we'll be here to protect you," assured her father. "Let's go outside and look at New York City and wait for the ferry that will take us there."

Outside Malka suddenly realized she had left her shawl inside. "My beautiful shawl," Malka wailed.

"Don't worry," her mother comforted her. "In the excitement you left it inside. Let's go look for it."

They went inside and looked all over. They went to all the places where they had been, but they could not find the shawl.

"What shall I do?" Malka sobbed. "It's cold and I need my shawl."

"You can huddle inside mine with me," her mother said. "When we get to New York City, Uncle Hershel will find something for you." She pulled Malka inside her shawl. Malka leaned against her mother and tried not to cry.

Going outside again Malka spotted her shawl on a railing. "Someone must have found it and put it there for its owner to find it," Malka's mother explained.

Malka's father took out his handkerchief and dried his daughter's wet cheeks. She meekly smiled up at him.

The ferry brought them in to New York City where her Uncle Hershel was waiting for them. After greeting each other and catching up on each other's news, they left for Uncle Hershel's apartment where they would be staying until Malka's father found a job and they could find an apartment of their own.

"I must apologize," Uncle Hershel said when they got to the building. "My apartment is small and the bathroom is in the hall for all the tenants to use, but it's home for now."

Opening the door, Uncle Hershel ushered them into a large room with a small kitchen nook. On the floor were four mattresses.

Malka wanted to complain but her father put his finger to his lips motioning her to be quiet.

"I just put the mattresses down this way," Uncle Hershel explained, "but I think Malka needs a place of her own."

"How?" asked Malka's mother.

"I have some clothes line," explained Uncle Hershel. "I will nail one end to the wall near the window and the other end between the two windows on the side wall. Then, if I may, I'll put one of your shawls on one line and the other shawl on the other line. I'll move one of the mattresses inside. Malka will have a private room."

"How kind of you," Malka's mother said, "but we're putting you to so much trouble."

"You're family," replied Uncle Hershel. "It's my pleasure."

That night as they sat around the table in the kitchen nook eating supper, Hershel told them about his job in a coat factory. "I think you can get a job there, too," addressing Malka's father. "And I think Malka can get a job modeling the coats for people and places who want to buy them," he added.

"She's only 13," replied Malka's mother. "She has to go to school yet."

"Hannah, in America girls her age are working already. If you want her to go to school there is night school."

That night Malka lay on her mattress crying softly. Her father pushed aside one of the shawls and sat down on the mattress next to her. He told her, "It will be all right. It's a new country. We'll get used to it."

Next morning Malka and her father went to work with Uncle Hershel to see if they could get jobs. Malka's mother stayed home to clean the room and make supper.

"We got the jobs," Malka's father said that afternoon when they got back. Malka wasn't too happy. "I want to go to school," she complained.

"You will in time," her mother said. "I will try to find a job too so we will make enough money and you won't have to work."

Malka's mother found a job in a nearby store but Malka was doing such a good job as a model of coats that she was given a raise, and her father wouldn't let her quit.

The more money we have the faster we will be able to get our own place. Then maybe you will not have to work."

In a few months they were able to find a three room apartment—with its own bathroom," her father crowed.

"You have a new coat now. What do you need that shawl for?" Malka's father asked his daughter when they were packing their belongings and gettingg ready to leave Uncle Hershel's apartment.

"I want to keep it. Can I, papa?" begged Malka.

"Let her," Malka's mother interrupted. "I'm keeping mine. It will be a remembrance of White Russia."

So the two shawls went to the new apartment. With the money they were making they were able to buy two beds.

"Who needs a living room?" commented Malka's mother. "Malka can have that for her own room. We can have our own bedroom."

"What are you going to do with the shawls?" Malka's father asked when he saw there wasn't room for everything in the small closet. "We don't need them anymore. Both Malka and you have coats now. Let's give them away.

"The shawls stay," Malka's mother insisted. "I think they will make lovely bedspreads for our new beds." So the shawls became bedspreads.

The following year Malka was still modeling coats but she still longed to go to school. One evening she went for a stroll in the neighborhood and spotted a school that had a night school.

"Can I enroll, please?" she begged her parents. "I want to go to school."

Her parents agreed and so at 14 Malka modeled coats by day and went to school at night. She was tired many days but she wanted to learn as much about America as she could.

One evening a young man enrolled in school. He said that he had recently come to America and was living with his uncle who managed a boarding house. His parents were still in Europe. They did not want to come to America. "I am helping my uncle around the house and he is paying me," he answered when Malka asked him if he had a job.

"I have a new friend," Malka announced to her parents one day.

"A boyfriend?" Malka's father questioned.

"Yes, pappa."

"Tell us about him," Malka's mother said.

"He is 16. His name is Israel Katz." Malka added, "I like him."

"You're 14 and he's 16." Malka's father was not too happy. "You are too young for a boyfriend."

"We're only friends," argued Malka.

"You can only see him in school. Do you understand?"

"Yes, pappa."

But Malka and Israel managed to see each other outside of school. They went on to finish their courses. When Malka was 16 and Israel was 18, they decided they wanted to get married.

Malka told her parents that decision one day.

"We haven't even met the boy yet. What is he going to do to support you?" Malka's father was angry with the news.

"We were about that age when we got married," Malka's mother reminded her husband.

"I had a job then," Malka's father said. "What is your young man going to do to support you?"

"His uncle wants to go back to Europe. He is leaving the boarding house to Israel. That's where we will live when we get married," explained Malka.

"And when will that be?"

"We are going to wait until I am 18. He'll be 20 then."

Malka and Israel didn't wait. Israel's uncle wanted to go back to Europe a few months later, so Malka and Israel eloped. Malka was almost 17.

When she told her parents, they didn't like it but there was nothing they could do so they gave the young couple their blessings.

Malka and Israel moved into the boarding house to become the managers.

"Take your shawl with you," Malka's mother insisted. "It's pretty and too nice to give away."

In their new place Malka packed the shawl in a box and put it away in a closet. She didn't know what to do with it. The beds already had spreads.

The following year Hannah and Joseph died in an automobile accident. When Malka had a baby girl they named her Hannah Josephine in honor of her parents.

Looking through the closet one day Malka came upon the shawl she had made in Russia. "This will make a lovely carriage cover," she told Israel. So the shawl was folded and tucked in around Hannah Josephine in the carriage whenever they went out.

When Hannah Jo, as she was called, outgrew the carriage the shawl was again used as a bedspread—this time on Hannah Jo's bed.

The boarding house grew into a hotel, and Israel was able to build a house for them on the hotel grounds.

The shawl moved with them and again became Hannah's bedspread.

One day when Hannah Jo was about four she was jumping up and down on her bed. Somehow a corner of the shawl got caught on the edge of the bed, and it tore.

"Mama, I tore the spread," she cried, going to find her mother.

"I'm sorry, Mama. I didn't mean it."

When Malka saw the spread she shrieked, "You naughty girl."

"I didn't mean it," Hannah repeated. "I'm sorry." Malka took the little girl by the and led her into the kitchen where she had been working.

"You are going to sit in the chair until your father comes home. Don't you dare get up," she said, putting Hannah Jo firmly in the chair at the kitchen table.

Hannah Jo put her head down and cried and cried.

"What's the matter?" Israel asked when he came home and saw Hannah Jo sitting at the table begging to get up.

When Malka told him, he said, "Let's go see the spread." Picking up Hannah Jo, up they went to the bedroom.

Israel inspected the spread. "This doesn't look too bad. The seamstress at the hotel can fix it. You'll never know it was torn." Addressing Hannah Jo he said, "It was an accident, wasn't it, honey?"

Hannah Jo shook her head.

"Apologize to your mother."

"I did already."

"Apologize again."

Hannah Jo whispered, "I'm sorry."

The seamstress crocheted a border of silver all around the torn spot. When it was returned, Malka complimented the seamstress. "That shawl is beautiful," she admired.

As Hannah Jo grew older, she wanted a different bedspread. Malka packed the bedspread into a sealed box and put it away where it stayed hidden for many years.

On Hannah Jo's wedding day it mysteriously appeared. Malka and Israel presented it to their daughter as a wedding present. "You and your husband Jacob can use it for your child," Hannah Jo's mother said as she presented it.

Before they had a baby, Hannah Jo and Jacob used the flowered shawl to decorate their living room couch. When their son Benjamin arrived, his carriage too was decorated with the shawl. When Benjamin outgrew the carriage, Malka said, "This is too pretty for a boy's bed."

"What are you going to do with it?" inquired Jacob.

"I don't know yet. I'll have it carefully cleaned and I'll put it away until I decided," answered Hannah Jo.

No one knew what happened to the shawl for many many years. Hannah Jo died suddenly without telling anyone where she had put the shawl.

Benjamin grew up, married Rachel, and had a daughter they named Malka in memory of her great grandmother.

One day when Malka was 16, her school was going to have a prom with an old fashioned clothes theme.

She asked her father is there was old fashioned clothes in Grampa Jacob's house.

"Ask him."

Malka went to her grandfather's house and asked if Grandma Hannah Jo had anything left from her mother.

"Your grandmother had some things her mother brought from Russia. I put them in the attic. You are welcome to go up and look."

Malka went upstairs and looked through the boxes that were there. In one box wrapped up in a cleaner's bag Malka saw something colorful.

Opening up the box she spied a big black shawl with colorful flowers and rimmed with silver. Running down the stairs she showed it to her grandfather.

"This is gorgeous," squealed Malka. "May I wear it?"

"Of course," Jacob replied. "Your grandmother would have been so happy to see you wear it."

"Tell me about it," Malka asked her grandfather.

So Jacob and Malka sat down on the living room couch and Jacob told his granddaughter the history of the shawl that came from Russia in 1912.

"Grampa," Malka said when he was finished, "when great grandma Malka made that shawl, little did she know her great granddaughter Malka would be wearing it, too."

"That's some family heirloom, isn't it?" Grampa Jacob smiled, kissing his granddaughter on the top of her head.

PART TWO

RUBBISH, THE GARBAGE DOG

Rubbish was a puppy with soft brown fur when he was found by the O'Day twins, Kara and Hara, when they brought trash from their home to the garbage dump. He had apparently been abandoned there, but had managed to survive on the food he had found there, because he was far from looking starved. The girls had brought him home and had named him Rubbish in honor of where they had found him.

Rubbish was always getting into trouble taking things out of the garbage can and inspecting and playing with them, and bringing home other people's garbage to his new home, too.

"That dog," said Mrs. O'Day in desperation one day as Rubbish brought some shells home, the garbage of a neighbor who had recently vacationed on the Rhode Island coast. "What shall we do with him?"

"Tie him up," said Mrs. O'Day. And so they did. Rubbish barked and protested but tied up he remained. Rubbish refused to eat or drink his water or play with the girls or their cousins, the Cunninghams, who came every day to see him and to play with him.

"He's so sad," said Hara one day after a week of this. "We have to do something or he will die if he doesn't eat. Can't we untie him?"

Mrs. O'Day gave in reluctantly. "We'll give him one more chance."

But Rubbish was happy to be untied and went right back to bringing his findings from the neighbors' trash back home.

"I give up," said Mrs. O'Day. "We must do something about this dog."

"Mom," said Hara, "since Rubbish loves garbage so much let's teach him to take out the garbage rather than bring it in. Then Kara and I won't have to do it anymore."

"Hooray for that," added Kara. "I'm all for less work for kids."

"I'm not," said their mother, "but if you can train Rubbish to take out the garbage, he won't get tied up again.

So the girls and their cousins began training Rubbish to take out the garbage. At first he just wanted to play, but in a few days he was bringing the bags out to the dumpster in the yard and depositing them in the proper receptacle. He was promptly rewarded with a pat and a treat each time he did what he was supposed to do. Rubbish was proud of himself, and the O'Days were proud of Rubbish.

It wasn't long before the men who loaded the garbage trucks let Rubbish help them whenever they came to pick up the garbage in the neighborhood. Soon the neighbors took notice, too. When they needed to have their garbage taken out, they'd bring it to their door and call Rubbish and he'd run to do that errant. And that's how he came to be called "Rubbish, the Garbage Dog."

J.P. CAT

J.C., Stacey, and Audie had a lot of fun playing with their cousin's dog, Rubbish, and Kara's kitten, Day, but they wanted a pet of their own. They asked their parents, who agreed if the girls promised that they'd take care of it properly. The three girls said they would, so the following Saturday Mrs. Cunningham took them to the Budd Hollow Animal Shelter.

The girls looked at all kinds of full-grown dogs, puppies, full-grown cats, and kittens, but none really appealed to them until they came to a small kitten with a big meow. The three fell in love with the kitten instantly and decided that that was the pet they wanted.

After their mother paid for it and the girls got instructions on its care, they headed for home, stopping at the grocery store for some cat food and kitty litter. When they got home, Stacey found two boxes and an old quilt in the basement, which their mother said they could have. The girls made a bed for the kitten from one box and filled the other with the kitty litter.

"What have you named him?" asked Hara when the O'Day twins came over later that day.

"Oh, my gosh, we haven't decided on a name yet," replied J.C.

"We've been so busy making the bed and litter box and trying to teach him to use the litter box that we haven't gotten to that yet."

"Let us help you with a name," suggested Kara.

"That's fine. What do you suggest?" asked Audie.

"How about Muffin?" thought Hara.

"Not the right ring," replied the Cunninghams.

"How about Puff, like the name of the cat in the readers in school?" suggested J.C.

"Too childish," said Audie.

"Noisy would be a good name," said Kara. "He's got a loud meow."

"Not right yet," said the others.

"Spot's a good name," said Kara.

"That's a dog's name," the others quickly followed.

"He's brown colored, so how about Brownie?" asked Audie.

"Not fancy enough," said the Cunningham twins.

"Let's ask Mom," said Audie. "Maybe she'll have a good idea."

"Mom," said the twins, "we're having trouble finding a good name for our kitten. Can you help us?"

"Why don't you call him Just Plain Cat—J. P. Cat for short?" suggested Mrs. Cunningham.

"That's positively elegant," the Budd Road Buddies said almost in chorus. "Mom, you're the greatest!" added Audie. "Thanks!"

The O'Day twins called their mom to tell her the news, then they all went outside to show J. P. Cat the neighborhood and introduce him to Rubbish and Day. Audie worried, "Do you think Rubbish will like him? Dogs and cats don't usually get along, even though Rubbish and Day don't bother each other."

"We'll soon see," said the others.

Kara called Rubbish, who came running. When he saw J. P. Cat, he stopped short, eyed him carefully, and then licked him all over. J. P. Cat responded by rubbing up against Rubbish.

"They like each other," shouted the Budd Road Buddies.

"Can you beat that?" added Mrs. O'Day, who had been watching from the porch. "I guess Rubbish, Day, and J. P. Cat are as unusual as their names," she said as she went back into the house.

KARA SAVES THE DAY

"Hurry up, slowpokes. We're wasting good swimming weather," Audie called out to her cousins, Hara and Kara, as she waited with her sisters, Stacey and J.C., and their mom near their station wagon in front of the Cunningham home on Budd Road.

"We're hurrying as fast as we can," Hara answered from the porch of the O'Day home across the street. "Mom will be out in a minute."

"Where are the Budd Road Buddies off to today?" asked their neighbor, Mrs. Smith, who overheard them while she was in her garden.

"We're going to Lazy River State Park with our Sunday School for the Budd Hollow Church picnic," replied Kara. "Our mother and Reverend and Mrs. Harland are coming, too."

"Have fun," Mrs. Smith said as she went back to pulling the weeds from her garden.

"Now let's get going," Audie said impatiently when the Johnsons came across the street.

"We're going. We're going," laughed her mom as the group piled into the car.

When they arrived, J.C. saw that the others were already at the picnic tables, so after the car was parked, the girls and their moms hurried over to where the group was sitting. Saying hi to everyone, the Budd Road Buddies and their moms sat down to eat, too.

After lunch, Reverend Harland suggested a softball game, the boys against the girls.

"We can beat you any day," Jimmy Jones teased the girls.

"Don't count on it," replied Stacey.

"There are more than eighteen of us," realized Tommy Davis. "How are we all going to play?"

"How about changing players every three innings?" suggested Reverend Harland. "That way, everyone will have a turn."

The children agreed that that was fair.

The boys won six to three.

"I told you we'd win," Tommy gleefully taunted the girls.

"You were just lucky. We'd beat you if we played again," Hara retorted.

"Sure, sure," Tommy added, running off to join the other boys who were heading for the basketball court.

"Boys," Audie said in exasperation, "let's go swimming. It's too hot to argue."

"Last one in is a rotten egg," Stacey called back to the other girls after they came out of the park's girls' locker room where they had gone to change.

"Take care," warned Mrs. Harland. "Stay where the lifeguards can see you, and don't tease Kara. Her mom said she is just learning to swim."

Seeing the girls in the water, the boys changed into their bathing suits in the boys' locker room and went swimming, too.

A few minutes later, Kara came out of the water and sat on the bank. Her mother came over and sat down with her.

"What's the matter, dear?" she asked.

"I don't swim well yet, and I just got tired."

"I'll sit with you, and we'll rest together."

Soon all the children came out and relaxed on the beach.

"I have a surprise for you," said Mrs. Harland when she saw that all the children were out of the water. "I made lemonade and oatmeal cookies this morning for an after-swimming treat."

As the children were sipping the drink and munching the cookies, a boy whom they all knew from Budd Hollow Central School, Dave South, rode up on his bicycle carrying a bag.

"What do you have in the bag?" asked Audie?

"A kitten," replied Dave. "I'm going to drown it, because I can't keep it and nobody else wants it."

"Are you crazy?" asked J.C., who was sitting next to Audie? "Why don't you give it to the animal shelter? They'd find a home for it."

"Too much bother," Dave answered. Without further discussion, he ran toward the water. The others watched in horror.

Before Dave reached the end of the beach, Kara, who was closest to the river, jumped up and ran into the water, reaching the bag just as it was going down.

While she was bringing it back, Dave ran back to his bike and drove off.

"That horrid boy," exclaimed Audie. "How could anyone do such a horrid thing?"

Kara opened the bag and brought out a tiny red ball of fur. "Oh, how pretty!" she said as she dried it with her towel.

"That was a very brave thing for someone who can't swim too well yet to do," said Reverend Harland to Kara.

"All I could think of when I saw Dave throwing the bag in were the words of Jesus, which I learned in church: 'Greater love hath no man than this, that a man lay down his life for his friends,'" said Kara, petting the kitten.

"It's nice to know someone listens to me," laughed Reverend Harland. Getting serious, he added, "I am very proud of you, Kara."

"What are we going to do with him?" Kara asked her mom.

Winking to the others, her mom replied, "Since Kara rescued it, perhaps she would like to keep it. That is, if she will take care of it."

"Will I? You bet! Thanks, Mom," Kara said, giving her mom a hug.

"What are you going to name your kitten?" J.C. asked her cousin.

Thinking for a minute, Kara said, "The Day I Found My New Friend."

"Isn't that a bit big for such a small kitty?" asked J.C.

Thinking again, Kara decided, "Well, then, I'll shorten it to just 'The Day.'"

While Kara continued to soothe her new pet, the children chanted "Hoorey, hooray, Kara, brave Kara, saves the day."

HARANDI, THE SAILBOAT
THAT NEVER SAILED

"Hey, you guys, wake up! The wind is fierce this morning. Just right for sailing," Kara yelled to her sister and cousins. Kara was up early the first morning of their week's vacation on Block Island, but the other Budd Road Buddies were still asleep. Mornings on Block Island are cool and good for sleeping.

Hara opened her eyes, yawned, and said to her twin, "What's the rush? This is vacation, and vacations are good for sleeping late."

"We're wasting good sailing weather," replied Kara.

"What's all the ruckus?" J.C. asked, coming from the next room.

"Time to go sailing," Kara once again answered. "Get Stacey and Audie."

J.C. went into the next room, which she shared with her twin and her older sister. "Get up! Get up!" she called.

"Why?" asked Audie, opening one eye reluctantly.

"Sailing time," chirped Kara as she shook Stacey awake.

The Budd Road Buddies were guests of their Aunt Diane and Uncle Harry, who had a summer home on Block Island. Their aunt and uncle owned a small sailboat called the *Harandi*, which was an anagram of their aunt's and uncle's names.

After a breakfast of juice, bacon and eggs, toast and milk, which Aunt Diane insisted they eat, the girls ran down to the dock where Uncle Harry was already working on the boat.

"It looks as if it's a bit too windy today for sailing," Uncle Harry said as the girls jumped into the boat.

"I thought wind is what makes sailboats go," said Hara.

"It does," said Uncle Harry, "but too much wind is not for little sailboats. Let's give it a try anyway," he said as he finished tying down the last of the sails.

As he began raising the sail, the wind blew it down furiously. He tried several times, but each time the wind blew down the sails. "Sorry to disappoint you, girls, but it is just too windy today. If we did go out, we'd jus capsize. Perhaps tomorrow."

Seeing their disappointment, Uncle Harry suggested a sightseeing trip around the island to see where Captain Adrian Block, for whom the island was named, first landed, where the Manisses Indians lived and are now buried, the famous Mohegan Bluffs, and the many fresh water ponds on this island, twelve miles from the Rhode Island shore and seven miles from Montauk, Long Island.

"Block Island is part of Rhode Island," Uncle Harry told the girls as they piled into his station wagon. "There are five hundred-fifty people who live here all year round. There's even a school with sixty pupils here on the Island."

Next day, the wind was just as fierce. "Looks like I have to disappoint you again," Uncle Harry told the girls when they came to the breakfast table.

"Is it always this windy here?" Audie asked her uncle.

"No," replied Uncle Harry. "It's usually very nice here for sailing."

"The wind must be angry with us," Kara said as she took a bite of her toast.

The others laughed.

"What shall we do today?" J.C. asked.

"I have some shopping to do on the mainland," said Aunt Diane.

"How about going over with me? We'll take the ferry across, along with our bicycles, and after I've bought what I need, we'll ride around Galilee, Narragansett, and Jerusalem, the fishing villages on the Rhode Island coast. I think you'd also like to see Point Judith, the lighthouse which is on the southernmost point of the land in Rhode Island."

The following day dawned bright and hot.

"I think we'd rather rest on the beach today and go swimming, too," Stacey said when Uncle Harry asked them if they wanted to go sailing that day.

"We're pooped from all that bicycle riding," added Audie. "We ride bicycles at home, but not as many miles as we did yesterday."

The day after that was just as hot, and the girls again preferred swimming and playing on the beach to sailing.

When the girls woke the following day, it was pouring rain.

"No sailing today, for sure," said Stacey. "Doesn't look as if we'll be going sailing this vacation."

"Wait until tomorrow, little Sis," said Audie.

But the next day brought more rain.

"There's just two days left," Hara said disappointedly. "It doesn't look as if we'll ever be going sailing."

"Perhaps tomorrow we can go," said Uncle Harry. "I'm so sorry things haven't worked out as far as sailing goes."

"Wish we could order good weather," lamented J.C.

"If wishes were horses, beggars would ride," the Budd Road Buddies chorused.

The next day, however, dawned dark and dreary, and rain was falling before noon.

"Can't understand this weather," said Uncle Harry. "We have so many good sailing days here. I don't know why the weather had to be so bad this week."

The day they were scheduled to leave for home, Uncle Harry said to the girls, "Some day, when the weather is very, very good early in the morning, I'll call you up and one of your dads can bring you up for the day. We are only a short trip from where you live, and there'd be plenty of time to go sailing, even if you had to go back home that night."

"Now, let's hurry, girls," said Aunt Diane, "so we won't miss the ferry."

Aunt Diane and Uncle Harry were taking the girls to the mainland, where Kara and Hara's dad would be meeting the girls to take them home.

"Do we have time to say good-bye to *Harandi*?" asked Stacey.

"Sure," said her uncle, "but don't be too long."

As the girls boarded the ferry with their aunt and uncle after saying good-bye to the boat, Hara asked, "Why couldn't sailboats be like ferries?"

"What do you mean?" asked Aunt Diane.

"Ferries rarely miss going out because of the weather. Why couldn't sailboats be like that?"

"That's a good question," laughed Uncle Harry.

Audie began chuckling to herself.

"What's so funny, Sis?" asked Stacey.

"I was just thinking that Gram is going to laugh when we tell her we couldn't go sailing because it was too windy."

"I've got an idea," said Uncle Harry. "How about adding to the boat's name the title 'The Sailboat That Never Sailed,' so we'll always remember this vacation?"

"*Harandi*, the Sailboat That Never Sailed," said Stacey aloud, trying out the sound. "That's got a good sound," she decided.

"How do you like it?" Stacey asked her sister and cousins.

"We love it," the Budd Road Buddies agreed. "Hooray for *Harandi*, the Sailboat That Never Sailed," they chanted as the other passengers smiled their approval.

GRANDMA CHEESE

J.C., Stacey, and Audie were playing tag with Kara and Hara on the front lawn of the O'Day home when Ashley Edwards arrived at her grandmother's house, which is next door to the O'Days on Budd Road. They waved as she walked inside with her suitcase.

"We'll unpack later," Grandma Edwards said to Ashley. "I want to introduce you to my neighbors."

Going outside, Mrs. Edwards called to the girls. When they came over, she said, "I want to introduce my granddaughter, Ashley Edwards. She is here for a week's vacation." Turning to Ashley, she said, "I would like you to meet J.C., Stacey, and Audie Cunningham and their cousins, Kara and Hara O'Day. Around here, we call them the Budd Road Buddies."

Ashley and the Budd Road Buddies said hi to each other.

Grandma said, "Ashley must be hungry and thirsty after her trip. It is too early for supper, but I am going to make her something to eat. Come inside, girls, and have something, too."

"I have to go inside and tell mom first," Kara said.

"Sit around the kitchen table while I fix the food." Ashley's grandmother invited the girls after they went into the Edwards' house.

As the girls chatted about their families and school, Mrs. Edwards set out a platter of American cheese slices and whole wheat crackers and six glasses which she filled with milk.

A half hour later, the girls left, thanking Mrs. Edwards for the treat.

Next day, the Cunninghams and the O'Days invited Ashley to go swimming with them at Lazy River State Park. That afternoon, Mrs. Edwards met them at the park, bringing with her Swiss cheese slices, rye crackers, a Thermos of milk, paper plates, paper cups, and napkins.

"Thought you girls would be starved after a day of swimming, so I brought you a snack," she said as she set out the food on the paper plates and put it at a picnic table under an oak tree near the beach area.

"Hits the spot," Ashley said as the girls hungrily ate everything on the plates. "Thanks, Gram."

Next day was a rainy day, Ashley invited the Budd Road Buddies to come to her grandmother's house for lunch and to play her favorite game, Monopoly. Over a lunch of macaroni and cheese and milk, the girls talked about what they wanted to be when they grew up. Audie said that she wanted to be a doctor. J.C. and Stacey wanted to be teachers. Kara and Hara didn't know what they wanted to be when they were older. Neither did Ashley.

The girls played together the rest of the week, and each afternoon, Ashley's grandmother gave them cheese, crackers, and milk.

Ashley's mom and dad were coming Saturday to take her home. The Budd Road Buddies had one last cheese treat with their newfound friend before she left. Seated around the Edwards' kitchen table, they exchanged addresses so they could write to each other until Ashley came for another visit.

"You certainly like cheese," Audie said to Mrs. Edwards as she again set out another platter of cheese and crackers and six glasses of milk.

"Yes, I do. I hope you do, too. It is full of calcium and protein. I eat some every day."

"We've enjoyed these afternoon treats," Hara said, popping one last slice of cheese into her mouth.

"Cover over any time, girls," Mrs. Edwards said as she collected the empty glasses to put into the sink.

As they were getting up, Kara said to Ashley's grandmother, "We have a friend who has a grandmother who likes to play golf. Everyone calls her Grandma Golf. We have another friend who has a grandmother who likes to sew. Everyone calls her Grandma Needle. Now, we have a friend whose grandmother likes to eat cheese. May we call you Grandma Cheese?"

THE SNAKE THAT GOT AWAY

Come one, come all
See our pets
Gym, Friday 2:00pm

Thus declared the poster on the bulletin board of the main lobby of Budd Hollow Central School.

On Friday, instead of the regular assembly, the school would be gathering in the gym to see the pets of the children of the elementary school. Each child would tell something about his pet. It would be a combination science and English presentation.

Promptly at 2:00pm on Friday the classes began filing into the gym. Kara and Hara brought their dog, Rubbish. Day stayed home. J.C. and Stacey brought J.P. Cat. Rebecca Cohen brought her goldfish in its tank. Billy Smith, who lived on a farm just outside of Budd Hollow, brought a snake in the box. He had found it in the woods and was keeping it as a pet after his father had said it was not a poisonous snake.

"That's a terrible pet," said Hara, who had just finished tying Rubbish's leash to one of the table legs.

"I like him," replied Billy. "It is interesting to watch him slither along."

"What's his name?" asked Kara.

"I call him Slinky," said Billy.

"What kind of snake is he?" asked Rebecca, who had just fed her goldfish.

"A garter snake. I'll tell you about the garter snakes during the program."

When the show began, the O'Day twins told how they had found Rubbish and how they had trained him. The Cunningham twins told how their cat acquired its name. Finally, it was Billy's turn. Billy told the students that snakes in general are legless, they "walk on their ribs" by having muscles move them along. His snake was a garter snake, which is not poisonous. It eats mice and insects by biting with teeth, not with tongues as most people think snakes do. Snakes taste and smell with their tongues, but do not bite with them. They do not have eyelids so their eyes are always open. Garter snakes do not lay eggs. They carry eggs in their bodies until the eggs develop into little snakes. The baby snakes are able to crawl about on their own from the beginning. Snakes shed their skins from time to time. A snake turns its old skin inside out as it crawls out of it. Snakes hibernate when cold weather comes.

After the show, the children went back to their classrooms. The pets were left on leashes or in boxes in the gym until dismissal. When the children were ready to go home, they went to get their pets, but Slinky was nowhere in sight.

The children looked everywhere—all around the gym, in the halls, all the classrooms, but Slinky could not be found.

"What shall we do? The bus has to leave," worried Kara.

Billy said, "If he's in the building, we'll find him Monday. If he's gotten out the door, it will be okay, because he will be in his natural environment."

"Don't you feel bad that you may not see Slinky again?" asked J.C.

"No. Snakes belong in the outdoors, not in a box. It was fun while it lasted. I was going to put him back in the grass soon anyway."

As the children were getting on the bus, Stacey said to Billy, "Maybe Slinky has a girl friend and wanted to go see her again."

"Could be," said Billy.

USHERING OUT THE QUEEN

"Why can't we go back by car?" Stacey asked when she and the other Budd Road Buddies arrived at Rebecca's house last Saturday before supper. The girls had been invited to spend Saturday evening with Rebecca and her parents at Temple Beth El, the synagogue in Budd Hollow.

"Because it is still the Sabbath," answered Rebecca, "and we do not ride on the Sabbath. Besides, it is not far from here, and the walk will be good for us. I go for a walk with my dad every Saturday when the weather is nice. It is our own little tradition."

"Let's go, girls," Rebecca's mother said when she was ready. "We do not want to be late for Havdalah!"

"What's that?" asked Audie.

"It's the service that separates the Sabbath from the rest of the week."

When Rebecca and the Budd Road Buddies arrived, they sat in the women's section.

The Rabbi put a silver cup in a saucer and filled it with wine until it overflowed. Then he said a prayer, said the blessing over the wine, and put the cup down. Next, he picked up a box shaped like a fish and filled it with spices. When it was filled, he put it down. After that he picked up a burning candle shaped like a braid and containing six wicks.

"That candle symbolizes the days of the week are separate from the Sabbath and that they are entwined apart from the Sabbath," Rebecca whispered to the girls.

The Rabbi next blessed the candle, picked up the cup of wine, said the blessing for the wine again, took a drink of the wine, put the cup down and put the flame of the candle out in the wine that had overflowed into the saucer.

The men who were present each went up, said the blessing over the wine, took a drink of wine, then wet their fingertips in the wine that was in the saucer and touched their eyes and pockets with their fingertips.

"That symbolizes their hope for good vision and good business all week," Rebecca quietly explained to the girls.

"Women don't drink from the Havdalah cup," Rebecca's mother answered when Kara wanted to know if they would be drinking form the cup, too.

The service concluded with the congregation singing a song dedicated to Elijah. When the song ended, Rebecca explained that Saturday night is associated with Elijah because Jewish tradition says that it will Elijah who would announce the arrival of the messiah, which will take place on the close of a Sabbath.

"In our religion, we believe that the messiah has arrived already in Jesus," said Kara.

"I know," said Rebecca, "but in our religion, we believe the messiah still has not come."

After they left the synagogue on the way to the social hall next door, Audie wanted to know why the men and women sat in different sections and not together.

"In the Conservative and Reform synagogues, the men and women do sit together, but this is an Orthodox synagogue, and by tradition the men and women sit apart from each other," replied Rebecca.

When they entered the social hall, they saw long tables set for dinner. "Now, we are going to have a big meal with all kinds of goodies," said Rebecca. "We'll spend the rest of the evening singing Israeli songs and dancing Israeli dances. I'll teach you the words to the songs and show you the dance steps so you can join in, too.

Later, Rebecca and her parents walked the Budd Road Buddies home. They thanked Rebecca and her mom and dad for inviting them, adding that they had a very enjoyable time and learned a lot.

As they were saying good night, Rebecca asked her friends if they knew they had just spent an evening with royalty. When they answered no, Rebecca went on. "The festivities we enjoyed this evening is our way of saying goodbye to the Sabbath until next week, but I think of it as escorting a first lady out the door. The Sabbath is considered the most important of all the Jewish holidays. For this reason, it is known as the queen of the holidays. The name for the evening we just spent in Hebrew is M'lava Malka. *M'lava* in Hebrew means 'ushering out.' *Malka* is a Hebrew name meaning 'queen.' Therefore, this evening you helped us in ushering out the queen."

EATING UNDER THE STARS

Come and eat with us in our hut

In which the roof will not be shut.
Wear something warm because an October night may be cold.
We'll be eating outside according to a tradition very old.

Declared the invitation the Budd Road Buddies received from their friend, Rebecca, to eat with her and her family Sunday evening.

"Isn't October too late for an evening picnic?" audie asked Rebecca.

"It isn't an evening picnic," replied Rebecca. "It is our Holiday of Huts, which we call Succoth. For eight nights we will each dinner in a small three-sided building which my father has built on the side of our house. It has no permanent roof, but we will decorate the ceiling with branches and leaves. My father has built an overhead door on hinges to close in case of rain. This building is called a *succah*. It is built against the side of the house to show it will not fall."

"Why do you celebrate this holiday?" asked Stacey.

"When the Jews fled Egypt in Biblical times, they wandered in the desert for forty years. During this time, they lived in four-sided houses to protect themselves from the sands and winds of the desert. They left the roof off so that there would be air in the building.

"Can you come?" Rebecca asked her friends after she finished her explanation.

"Yes, of course," said Hara. "Our parents said we could, and we always enjoy sharing your holidays with you."

When the girls arrived on Sunday, they saw apples, bananas, pears, grapes, cucumbers, tomatoes, celery, and beets hanging from the ceiling of the succah on strings. On the walls were pictures of different kinds of branches.

"The fruits and vegetables are in honor of the harvest in Israel, where farmers use these four-sided buildings in the fields because they are easy to construct. Succoth is very much like Thanksgiving. We give thanks for the food that has been grown," Rebecca told her friends when they wanted to know why the fruits and vegetables were hanging from the ceiling and the pictures were on the walls.

"About the pictures," Rebecca continued, "these branches are used in the celebration of Succoth. The branch of the citron fruit is called the Ethrog. It symbolizes educated people who do good deeds. The branch of the palm tree is called Lulav and symbolizes people of great wealth but who do not do good deeds. The branch of the myrtle is called Hadas and symbolizes educated people who do not use their knowledge to benefit people. The branch of the willow is called Aravah. It symbolizes people without money, knowledge, or good deeds."

Rebecca's father conducted a service before dinner. He put in his right hand three myrtles, two willows, and one *ethrog*, bound by a *lulav*. In his left hand he held an *ethrog* and *lulav*. He pointed these branches east, west, north, south, up, and down.

"Up and down symbolizes Earth and Heaven," Rebecca explained. "My dad holds the branches together to show the unity of all people. He moves them in all directions to signify that God rules over all of us from all directions."

While Rebecca's mother was serving dinner, J.C. looked up. Through the branches she saw the sky. It was clear and bright. A big full moon was shining. "Look," she said. "What a beautiful night. We are eating dinner under the stars."

FINDING THE AFIKOMEN

Kara walked into the Cunningham house after she and Hara had dropped off their books on their return from the library one Saturday morning just before the Passover/ Easter spring vacation from school.

"We were invited to Rebecca's house for their Passover Sedar," she said to Audie, who was busy cleaning J.P. Cat's litter box.

"So were we," replied Audie. "Are you going?"

"You bet. Are you?"

"Yup."

Rebecca Cohen lives up the street from the Budd Road Buddies and is also ten and in fourth grade. The girls have been friends for many years and Rebecca is unofficially one of the Budd Road Buddies.

After Audie finished cleaning and changing the litter box, she and Kara went outside where the other girls were playing with Rubbish, Kara and Hara's dog.

"What shall we do today?" asked J.C. when Rubbish got tired of playing and ran off.

"Let's go up to Rebecca's house and find out more about their sedar," suggested Stacey. "She's home now."

"Hello," said Mrs. Cohen when she answered the door and found the Budd Road Buddies on the porch. "Rebecca's in her room. Go on in."

"Hi, gang," Rebecca said when the girls entered her room.

"Hi, Beck," said Audie. "We want to know more about your sedar, and we thought this might be a good time for you to tell us."

"Make yourself comfortable," replied Rebecca.

As the girls sprawled on the floor, Rebecca's bed and on her lounge chair, Rebecca began her story.

The sedar is a special meal served with special foods. It symbolizes the Jews' freedom from Egyptian bondage. Actually, it is a combination service and meal. We read from a book called the Haggadah. The part, I think, you'll like best is the game we play during the dinner. It is called *Finding the Afikomen*. I'll explain that in a minute. First things first.

The table has to be set in a certain way. In the center of the table is a large platter on which a roasted shank bone, a roasted egg, a dish of horseradish, a dish of lettuce, and a dish of a mixture of apples, nuts and wine are set on it and there is a napkin folded over three times with three matzohs in it. A decanter of wine with glasses for each plus one extra for Elizah is set out.

"Why all these things?" interrupted Hara.

"I'll explain soon," continued Rebecca. "Let me finish telling you how the table has to be set first."

"A pillow is set to the left of the chair of the head of the house. That's my father, of course. And a large bowl, a towel, and a pitcher of water is put near the table. Now to explain. The shank bone symbolizes the animal sacrifices made on the altar of the great Temple in Jerusalem on the Passover. The egg is a symbol of the festival offering made on Pesach, Shavous, and Succoss. The horseradish reminds us of the bitterness of slavery. The mixture of apples and nuts and wine is a symbol of the mortar made into bricks by the Jews when they were slaves in Egypt. The lettuce symbolizes the spring season in which Passover occurs. The matzohs are the unleavened cakes made by the Jews as they fled Egypt. The three layers represent the three main groups of Jewish people—Kohen, Levi and Yisroel. They are placed together to indicate the unity of the Jewish people. It is the middle matzoh that will be hidden and must be found. I'll explain that later."

"We must drink four cups of wine during the evening at definite times."

"We're too young to drink wine," interrupted J.C.

"Not to worry. The children drink grape juice instead," continued Rebecca.

"What's the extra cup for?" asked Audie.

"It's for Elijah, the prophet, who is the bearer of good tidings, according to legend. He comes to everyone's Sedar after the meal to symbolize freedom and peace for all men during the coming year. We open the door to welcome him after the meal. Legend says he will come in, drink his wine and leave."

"You didn't tell us about the pillow yet," said Kara impatiently.

"Give me a chance," said Rebecca. "The pillow symbolizes freedom, too. In Biblical times only free men were allowed to relax during a meal. In fact, it was a sign of freedom if he reclined during the meal. At the meal, we're allowed to slouch at the table."

"We'd get killed if we did that at home," said Audie.

"So would I, ordinarily," said Rebecca, "but at the Sedar it is part of the evening."

"We do not eat right away when we sit down," continued Rebecca. "There is a certain order to the way we do things. First, we drink the first cup of wine with its blessing. Then, we wash our hands also with its blessing. That's what the bowl, pitcher and towel are for, by the way. Then we eat the lettuce. Then comes the part you will like. My father will take the middle matzoh, called Afikomen, and hide it in its special napkin. Whoever finds it by the end of the meal gets an award. Next, the youngest child asks what is called the Four Questions and the story of how Passover came about it told. I'll be asking this year, by the way, and my father will tell us the story. Next comes the second cup of wine, another ritual hand washing, ritual tasting of the horseradish, and finally, the main part of the meal is served. After the meal, whoever has found the Afikomen brings it out, is promised an award to be given after the holiday since money is not allowed during the holiday, and then the Afikomen is eaten. Tradition says the Afikomen must be eaten in silence. Then we have our third cup of wine and the door is opened for Elijah. Our fourth cup completes the meal. The rest of the evening is devoted to songs and stories about the Jews' flight from slavery.

"Do you think you'll enjoy it?" Rebecca asked when she finished all of her explanations.

"Sounds very interesting," agreed the Budd Road Buddies.

"I am so glad you will be coming. Holidays are more meaningful when they are shared with friends," Rebecca said as she said goodbye at the front door when the girls had to go home.

As the Budd Road Buddies walked along on their way home, they wondered who would be *Finding the Afikomen.*

PART THREE

MA, I DON'T WANNA GO

Adam's mother waited outside his school in Old Palms, Florida. She had attended the Christmas play Adam's fourth grade had presented on this last day of school before Christmas vacation. She was going to be taking him to a five-day baseball camp for boys. Even though the camp was not far from their home, Adam was going to be sleeping over. His suitcase was in the trunk of her car, packed and ready to go.

As soon as the dismissal bell rang, children began running out the front door. When Adam came out, he saw his mother, and got into the car, and off they headed to the camp. But Adam did not look happy.

"Why so glum?" his mother asked.

"I don't wanna go to camp," Adam complained.

"Why not?" asked his mother. "You love baseball. That's why your Aunt Harriet bought you a session at camp for a Christmas present.

"But I wanna be home for Christmas," Adam whined.

"You will be. The camp is over the day before Christmas."

Reluctantly Adam agreed to try it for one day after his mother promised to bring him home the following day if he didn't like it.

They arrived at the camp just ahead of the shuttle buses which were bringing boys who had flown in from other parts of the country to the nearby airport.

"Don't forget to call me tomorrow," Adam reminded his mom when he got out of the car.

"I won't forget," his mother replied.

Adam took his suitcase out of the trunk of the car and looked around trying to figure out where he had to go. He looked frightened.

His mother offered to go with him to find out where he had to go, but Adam refused.

"No, Ma, don't. Everyone will think I'm a baby."

But she watched from her car and didn't drive away until a tall muscular man with a flat top haircut came and introduced himself to Adam.

"Hi, I'm Clint Hurdle. I'm the director of the camp. What's your name?"

"My name is Adam."

"Put it there, Adam," Clint said extending his hand to shake hands with the boy.

Shaking hands Adam wanted to know what he should call the director.

"Call me by my first name."

"OK, Clint."

"Actually that's my middle name. My first name is Mr."

Adam looked puzzled. Clint laughed.

"Call me Clint or Mr. Hurdle but please don't call me late for lunch."

"Looking at his clipboard Clint told Adam that he would be rooming with Alex and Aaron who were also in the fourth grade.

"I'll show you to your room."

When they got to the room, Clint showed Adam which bed and dresser was his and told him to unpack. Then he said he had to leave to greet the other campers.

Fifteen minutes later he was back with two boys.

"Adam, meet your roommates Aaron and Alex."

The boys said "hi" and shook hands. Then Aaron and Alex were shown which beds and dressers were theirs and were told to unpack.

"Be in the auditorium at 4:30," Clint said before he left.

"Where are you from?" Adam asked his roommates. Aaron said that he was from New York City. Alex said that he was from Chicago.

"Where are you from?" Alex asked Adam.

"About twenty miles from here," Adam replied, "but I am going to be sleeping here rather than going home every night."

"How come your parents let you come so far?" Adam asked both boys. Alex said that his parents came down on the plan with him, but they were going to be vacationing in the area while he was in camp. Aaron said that his parents came down on the plane with him, too, and they would be visiting with his grandparents until camp was over.

The boys told each other what positions they played. Adam was a pitcher. Alex played first base. Aaron played right field.

After all three boys were finished putting their clothes away, they decided to look around.

"We have time until it is time to go to the auditorium," Aaron said looking at his watch.

Walking around they saw the baseball fields, the batting cages, the building where their dining room was, and the building where the auditorium was. And they met other campers looking around, too.

Glancing at his watch again Aaron said, "It is 4:15. We better head for the auditorium. We don't want to be late."

On a table beside the door to the auditorium was a large table with tee shirts on it. A sign read TAKE ONE. When the boys took theirs and unfolded them, they saw that the camp's name was on it.

After everyone was seated, Clint welcomed the group and introduced the staff explaining that each one was a coach or instructor with one of the major league baseball teams. Adam realized that the New York Mets, Chicago White Sox, Cleveland Indians and Kansas City Royals were represented and breathed a deep, "Wow."

"Boys," Clint went on, "I want to tell you the schedule for this week."

"Don't call us boys," one teenager in the back yelled.

"All right then," Clint began again, "Young people of the male gender." Everyone laughed. "We get up at seven o'clock and I do mean get up. We have a very busy day and we have to start early."

Someone in the back yelled out, "What happens if we don't get up at seven?"

"When you get up, we make you go play with the girls in their camp down the road from here."

"Ugh," groaned the younger boys. The older boys gave each other high fives.

"OK, OK," Clint went on. "You can stay but you'll have to eat spinach three times a day. Now let's settle down so I can tell you about what we'll be doing this week."

The boys—oops, young people of the male gender—learned that there would be individual instructions in batting, hitting, and fielding and there would be group instructions, too.

Clint ended, "For the next five days you'll be eating, sleeping, and breathing baseball."

"It's dinner time now so let's go to the dining room," Clint added at the end. After dinner you may go to the recreation room. We have a television, video games, and a pool table. You may stay there until bedtime which is nine o'clock."

"What?" gasped the group. "Why so early?" one of the boys asked. "We're not babies."

"Because I said so," replied Clint. "Actually beginning tomorrow we will be having evening sessions, and you'll be very happy to be in bed by that time."

Promptly at nine, Clint told the boys to go to their rooms.

"Party pooper," the boys complained as they headed to their rooms.

But they did not go to sleep. They stayed up talking.

"Boys," Clint yelled going from room to room. "Go to sleep. I need my beauty rest. If you don't go to sleep now, I'll come tuck you in and sing you a lullaby."

"Please don't," one of the coaches begged. "That's too much punishment."

At breakfast the next morning Clint had a confession.

"It says in our brochures that our meals are outstanding, but I'm sorry to say we'll have to eat them inside sitting down."

By that time Adam, Alex and Aaron had already become fast friends. Earlier that morning they had made a sign for their door THIS WAY TO THE THREE A'S.

When Adam's mom called after breakfast, Adam told her that he had decided to stay.

The staff worked with the older boys while Clint worked with the younger boys. With calm but firm teaching, all the boys did improve their skills. On the last evening of camp the boys divided up into teams and played each other in three inning games.

"Why can't we play more innings?" one of the boys asked.

"Mainly because we don't have enough space and besides you have to start packing to go home," was Clint's reply.

"Shucks," the boy complained.

In the morning of the last day, the shuttle buses arrived around ten o'clock to take the boys back to the airport.

"My parents are meeting me there," Aaron explained when Adam asked him where his parents were going to meet him.

"Same here," said Alex. "When is your mom coming?" Alex asked his new friend.

"She'll be here soon."

They exchanged addresses and promised to write to each other. They hoped they would be allowed to come to camp again.

Clint and the rest of the staff said goodbye to each of the boys and thanked them for coming.

"I hope you can come again next year," Clint said as he shook each boy's hand.

Adam, Alex and Aaron hung back, not wanting to part. Finally, Alex and Aaron had to get on the bus.

"Remember we'll always be the three A's," Alex shouted out the bus window to Adam after he and Alex had gotten on the bus.

Adam waved to them until the bus pulled away.

By the time all the buses had pulled out, Adam's mom arrived. Adam slowly got into the car.

"What's the matter?" his mother asked. "You look sad."

"I had a great time, Ma. I don't wanna go home."

PART FOUR

DAVIE'S ACCOMPLISHMENT

"Do you have your bat?" Davie's mother asked her eight year old son. She was helping him pack for a week at a baseball camp for boys 8-12.

"Yes, ma," replied Davie. "I also have my gloves, cleats, and Little League cap."

"The list we got from the camp said that you also need toothbrush, toothpaste, comb, shampoo and pajamas as well as two pair jeans, two T-shirts, two sets underwear, and two pair socks." Davie's mother went on, "Let me see what you have set out to pack."

After she checked everything she declared that they had everything. She helped Davie put it in his gym bag and backpack.

The next morning bright and early they left. Davie's mother was going to drop him off, check to make sure he was unpacked, then leave. She would pick him up the following week.

When they arrived at the camp, they found that they were the first there, so they looked around until they could find someone who could show them where the bunkhouse was.

Suddenly a tall man wearing a cowboy hat came out of a nearby building. "Hi," he said, extending his hand to Davie's mother. "I'm the director. My name is Clint."

Shaking Davie's hand he said, "Or you can call me Mr. Clint. Or you can call me Baseball Guy. But you cannot call me late for lunch."

"This sounds like it's going to be a fun week," Davie's mother said to her son as they were unpacking in the bunk that Clint had shown them.

"I'll stay with you until the others come," Davie's mother said, "so you won't be alone."

Before long the other boys came, and Davie's mother met the other parents.

"Goodbye, ma," Davie urged when she remained after the other parents had left. He didn't want the other guys to think he was a baby.

"See you next week," Davie's mother said as she left to go back home.

The boys chatted, mostly about baseball, until they heard a voice over the loudspeaker. "Gentlemen, it is now time for supper. The food here is outstanding but we are going to eat it inside sitting down."

The boys groaned and rolled their eyes.

At supper the boys were introduced to the staff who would be teaching them all week. After everyone was finished eating, they all talked baseball some more. The boys were excited that their teachers had been in the big leagues.

Soon it was bedtime. After the boys had showered, brushed their teeth and gotten into their pajamas, they hopped into their bunks. They were tired but baseball camp means baseball talk, so they talked some more—sharing their experience and sharing who their favorite big league players were.

The door of the bunkhouse opened. Clint was standing there. "Gentlemen, bedtime means sleep. So go to sleep." With that he turned off the lights and left.

The boys giggled in the dark.

The door opened again. "Gentlemen," Clint said, "If you don't go to sleep, I'll have to sing to you."

"Please don't sing," begged the boys. "We'll sleep."

The next morning after breakfast the boys gathered on the field. They were grouped according to age and were told that the eight year olds would play against the eight year olds, the nine year olds would play against the nine year olds, etc.

"Gentlemen," Clint went on, "This camp will be like the players in the big leagues train. That means first everyone exercises."

"Everyone around the track once," he ordered.

When the boys returned panting because it was a big league track, Clint said, "Now we're going to do some aerobics."

"Are you still alive?" Clint joked after five minutes.

"OK, now the fun begins. Every day you are going to get instructions in batting, running, catching and sliding. There are enough here so each age group can make up two teams. Every day each group will play against each other for three innings. At the end of the week each age group will play against each other for seven innings. Now let's get going."

Each day the boys followed that routine.

One group of eight year olds called themselves THE ATOMS. The other group called themselves THE CYCLONES. Davie was on THE CYCLONES. THE ATOMS were designated the visiting team, THE CYCLONES the home team.

The three inning games though short were fiercely played. On the last day Davie was assigned to play second base.

THE ATOMS scored first making it a 1-0 game, but THE CYCLONES tied it up in the bottom of the inning. It stayed that way until the sixth inning when THE ATOMS scored again. Now the score was 2-1 in favor of THE ATOMS. In the bottom of the sixth, THE CYCLONES scored two runs making the score 3-2 in favor of THE CYCLONES. In the top of the seventh, the first batter hit a single. The second batter hit a single. Now there were two batters on base. The next batter hit a line drive—right into Davie's mitt. Thinking that would be a hit, the runners had taken off for the next base. But before they could get to their base, Davie quickly tugged the runner between second and third, turned around and quickly tagged the runner between first and second. Davie had made an unassisted triple play.

No one could believe it at first. Then everybody from all the teams ran to Davie and everybody was high-fiving everybody else.

After they had almost trampled each other in the way baseball players congratulate each other, Clint broke through and shook Davie's hand. "Do you know what you just did?"

Davie shook his head not understanding what Clint meant.

"You did something that is very rare in the major leagues. I'm very proud of you. You should be proud of yourself, too."

Davie just felt embarrassed. It had not quite sunk in what he had done.

"Wait till next year," THE ATOMS players warned when all the boys left the field.

"That's a go," THE CYCLONES challenged.

When Davie's mother came to pick them up later that day, she saw a banner above the door of the bunkhouse that read WAY TO GO, DAVIE!!

"What's all that about?" Davie's mom asked Clint while she was waiting for Davie to say goodbye to his new friends.

And Clint told her about DAVIE'S ACCOMPLISHMENT.

PART FIVE

A DEER NAMED VELVET

Ashley saw them first. "What's that?" she asked her friends Adam and Alex as the three waited for the school bus one sunny spring morning. They lived in the country three miles from school and had to go to and from school by bus. All three were in fourth grade.

"What's what?" Adam asked.

Ashley pointed to the apple tree where two brown animals rested beneath the tree.

"I don't see anything," replied Adam at first, but after looking hard in the direction of the tree, he changed his mind. "It looks like a mother deer and a baby deer."

"Let's not bother them," Ashley said quietly.

"We don't have time anyway," said Alex. "Here comes the bus."

When the three got to their classroom, they excitedly told their teacher, Miss Clinton, about their discovery.

"The mother deer is called a doe," explained Miss Clinton, "and the baby is called a fawn. Don't touch the baby or disturb the mother."

"We won't," the children promised.

Later that day the class went to the library. "Would you like to learn more about deer?" Miss Clinton asked Ashley, Adam, and Alex. They did. Miss Clinton took a D book from an encyclopedia set that was on the reference book shelf and turned to the section on deer. She read to the children that fawns are born in the spring. The mother protects the baby from harm by hiding it in the grass and bushes where its color blends into the surroundings, making the baby hard to be seen. Miss Clinton went on reading that male deer are called bucks. Only the males have antlers, which begin growing in the spring and are fully grown by fall. the antlers begin to decay then and fall off by winter. New antlers are grown every year.

"How are the antlers grown?" Alex wanted to know. Miss Clinton read on that the antlers are bony tissue and covered with hairy skin called velvet while they are developing. The velvet is the nourishment. When the antlers are fully grown, the velvet is no longer needed, and the bucks rub the hairy skin off on trees and rocks.

When Ashley, Adam and Alex got home from school that afternoon, they looked under the apple tree. The mother and baby deer were still there. Another deer was there too.

"That must be the daddy," said Ashley.

"He's called a buck," Adam reminded her.

The next morning the children asked Miss Clinton if they could learn more about deer.

"That's a very good idea," agreed their teacher. "When you are finished, would you like to share the information with the rest of the class?"

"Of course," said Ashley.

Ashley, Adam and Alex spent their free time the next few days in the library reading everything they could find on the subject of deer. They took careful notes so that they could tell their classmates what they had read.

They told their classmates that deer are cud-chewing just as cows are. Deer, like cows, eat vegetation. Apples is one of the deer's favorite food.

One of their classmates asked what kind of deer was under the apple tree by the bus stop.

"White tail deer," answered Ashley. "In the eastern part of the United States this is the kind most found."

"Why are they called that?" their classmates wanted to know.

"Because when they run their talks stand straight up and the white color on the underside of their tails can be seen. The top side is brown and the bottom side is white, but it is only when they run that the white can be seen," Ashley explained.

Another one of their classmates wanted to know what other animals were in the deer family.

"In the western part of the United States the deer are called mule deer," explained Alex. They are smaller than white tail deer and look like mules.

Alex went on. "Other members of the deer family are caribou, elk, moose, and reindeer. Caribou and reindeer are different in that both male and female have antlers." Caribou may be white to blend in with the snow of the far north where they live.

"How big are the deer?" one of the girls in the class asked.

"White tail deer are four feet tall. Mule deer a little smaller. Elk are about five feet tall. Moose are the largest members of the deer family," Ashley explained. "They are over seven feet tall, can weigh 1800 pounds, can have legs four feet long, and its antlers can weigh 60 pounds."

"No one has mentioned anything about how fast deer can run," one of the boys remarked.

"I can tell you that," said Alex. "White tail deer can run forty miles an hour and can leap fifteen to twenty feet at a time. The larger the deer the slower they go. Moose can only run about twenty miles an hour."

"You did an excellent job," Miss Clinton complimented the children when they were finished. "I have a question I bet you can't answer. What's another name for the white tail deer?"

The class was silent while Ashley, Adam and Alex thought and thought. Finally they said, almost in unison, "We give up."

"Virginia deer," replied their teacher. "Can you tell me why?"

"Because they came from Virginia?" Ashley asked.

"You're right," Miss Clinton said. "They originally came from that state."

The deer family remained under the tree and in the fields near the bus stop. Every day Ashley, Adam and Alex watched them. The fawn stood on shaky legs at first but soon was strong enough to run with his father and mother into the woods and back again.

One day Ashley decided, "Even though we can't touch them, I think we should give them names."

"That's silly," said Alex.

"At least the baby?" Ashley begged.

"OK! OK!" agreed the boys. "What do you want to call it?"

Ashley thought for a minute. "How about Velvet?" she finally asked.

"What?" chorused the boys.

"Do you remember what we learned about how the antlers are formed?"

When the boys remembered themselves about what the hairy skin is called, they understood where Ashley got the name.

"OK! Velvet it is. The fawn looks soft like velvet anyway," the boys conceded.

All summer the children watched the deer family romp in the fields during the day and bed down at night under the apple tree. By the time school began in September, Velvet was big. Still the family stayed together.

One day in October when the children came out to wait for the school bus, they did not see the deer.

"Maybe they went into the woods early," Ashley worried.

On their return from school, the children still could not see the deer. Nighttime came. Still no deer. "Where could they be?" Ashley worried, more distressed than before. "I hope they did not get hurt."

A few days went by but the deer never came back. "What could have happened to them?" Ashley cried to the teacher.

They probably went into the woods to start a new family." Miss Clinton comforted her. "You'll probably see them again next spring with their new fawn. Don't worry, dear, they'll be back."

"I will have to think of a name for the new baby," Ashley said, wiping the tears from her eyes. "Do you have any ideas for a name?" Ashley asked her teacher.

"We have all winter to think of one," Miss Clinton said gently, smiling at the girl as Ashley went back to her desk feeling happier thinking about the deer coming back next year.

PART SIX

CAT'S IN THE DOG HOUSE

Just Plain Cat is long for J.P. Cat, the name Ashley gave her grey and white kitten, but she calls it Cat for short. Ashley lives with her mom and dad on a farm. They also have a big, brown dog named Dawg, which is not long or short for anything.

One summer day, Ashley and her mom were sitting at the picnic table in their front yard, rolling up a skein of blue yarn. Ashley's mother wanted to knit a sweater for Ashley. Cat was sitting near them trying to catch the yarn as they worked.

"Watch out that the kitten doesn't get the yarn and drag it on the ground," warned Ashley's mom. "We don't want it to get dirty."

When they finished, Ashley's mom got up, put the ball of yarn on the chair, and went inside to get some lemonade and cookies so that they could have a snack.

Ashley played with her kitten, warning it not to touch the yarn, but the naughty kitten did not listen. She caught one end in her paw. As Ashley tried to get it off, Dawg came around the corner of the house. Seeing the dog, the cat became frightened and ran off, dragging the yarn behind her. Dawg was too hot to run after her. He just wanted to lie in the shade under the picnic table.

"Cat!" yelled Ashley. "Come back. Dawg is not chasing you. Dawg, go away so Cat will come back."

Dawg got up, shrugged, and went back around the house.

Hearing the commotion, Ashley's mom hurried out of the house. "What happened?" she asked. But when she saw that the cat was gone and that the yarn was strung along the grass and all in a heap where it finally came off the cat's paw, she guessed.

"That cat is going to be in the dog house when I find her."

"What does that mean?" Ashley asked her mom.

"It's a saying your grandmother used. I would be in trouble if I did something wrong," explained Ashley's mom.

"Will Cat be in trouble?" worried Ashley.

"No," replied her mom.

"I'll scold her but since she is just a kitten, and kittens like to play with string, I will not stay angry with her.

"Help me pick up the yarn. We'll reroll it after we have our snack." After they picked it up, Ashley's mom took it inside and brought out a tray on which were two glasses, a pitcher of lemonade, and a plate of oatmeal cookies, which she had baked that morning.

It was too hot to sit at the picnic table, so they sat on the grass under the maple tree, which was nearby, as they ate their treat. The cool lemonade tasted good on such a hot day.

Neither Cat nor Dawg came back to the front yard. After they finished eating, Ashley said, "Let's go find Cat and Dawg."

Ashley and her mom went looking for their pets. They looked in the barn. They looked in the garage. They looked in the basement. They even looked inside the house. But they could not find them anywhere.

"Let's look in Dawg's house," suggested Ashley.

"Cats and dogs don't get along with each other too well. I don't think we'll find them there," her mom said.

"Let's look anyway," Ashley insisted.

They went to the back porch where Ashley's dad had built a house for Dawg. Ashley peeked in. Cat and Dawg were curled up, taking a nap together.

"Isn't that something?" said Ashley's mom. "It looks as if our pets like each other and are going to be friends."

Ashley laughed. "Mom, you said that the cat would be in the dog house when you find her, and sure enough, that's where J.P. Cat is."

PART SEVEN

JUDY'S SON

PART I

Beads of sweat rolled down my face and my blonde hair hung limply as I worked. It was the last day of school at White Lake High School, and I was cleaning out my desk and my closet. I had been teaching social studies for the last three years but I would not be returning in September. The students had already been dismissed, so I worked leisurely. I opened the windows hoping to get a little breeze. Then I thought perhaps that wasn't such a good idea. "My skin is fair and I burn easily," I thought to myself. "Maybe I better put on some sun blocker." Reaching into my pocketbook, I pulled out a tube and smoothed some of the cold cream onto my face and arms.

"What kind of surprise is this? What do you mean you're going home to Longwood and not coming back in September? When did you plan to tell me?"

Without looking up I knew it was the science teacher whose room was across the hall. I loved this big Black man whom I met when I first came to White Lake. We had been talking about getting married. But I was urged by well-meaning friends to rethink my decision because interracial marriages were still looked upon with disdain. And I did rethink the decision and realized marriage would not be a good idea.

"You heard right, Tom. I am leaving. I didn't tell you because I thought that by your hearing it through the grapevine, you'd get angry at me and wouldn't mind my leaving. I am going back to Longwood. My father told me in his last letter that there is an opening in the social studies department at Longwood High. I applied and have been accepted."

"You're talking nonsense. When did you decide this? Why didn't you discuss this with me?" Tom was fighting to keep his composure, but wasn't being too successful.

"I've been agonizing over it for a long time. I've looked at it from all angles. Getting married just won't work. I love you and want to marry you, but there is still too much prejudice against interracial marriages, especially in a small town like this place. Perhaps we could make a go of it but if we have children they would have big problems. I am leaving because I can't stand remaining here and seeing you every day, knowing what could have been if the world was more understanding."

"Honey, we could make marriage work," Tom pleaded. "We wouldn't be the first interracial couple to marry. Even if we were, we'd find a way."

I turned away. I didn't want Tom to see the tears beginning to slide down my cheeks. "My mind is made up," I finally uttered. "Find yourself a nice Black girl and get married."

"I don't want to find myself a nice Black girl. I want to get married to you. Why didn't you discuss this with me?"

"Tom, I can't stand this anymore. Please leave."

"Can I at least kiss you goodbye?"

"No, just leave."

Tom left slamming the door behind him. I blew him a kiss and whispered, "I'll always love you, Tom Desmond."

I went back to my work, finishing by putting my nameplate, JUDY MANN, on the last box.

In the fall Tom returned to White Lake High School. Memories were everywhere. He couldn't concentrate on his work or his life. He handed in his resignation to become effective at the end of the term in January. He returned to Atlanta where he had previously taught. He applied for a full-time job in several schools, but since there would be no openings until the fall, he signed up to do substitute teaching for the rest of the term. He was terribly lonely. Weekends were especially hard. To fill his lonely hours he volunteered time at Mid City Children's Hospital.

It was here he met Larissa Blake, a tall Black good-looking nurse at the hospital. They began dating. When Tom told her about my decision, she agreed, which surprised Tom. "Biracial children are not accepted," Larissa explained. "I see it in the hospital all the time."

"Why should it make a difference?" Tom asked.

"It shouldn't but it does," replied Larissa. "Maybe someday the world will be more accepting."

One day in March Tom surprised Larissa. "We've only known each other a short time, but I think I love you and I want to marry you. Will you marry me?"

Larissa accepted even though she knew Tom was still bitter over my refusal. "Try not to be bitter, Tom. We'll have a good life together. You'll see."

"Let's set the date for May. School will be over then and we'll have time for a long honeymoon. That is if you can take time off then."

"I get four weeks vacation so I can easily arrange to take it in May."

"Enough talk, the future Mrs. Tom Desmond. How about a kiss?"

They settled down to make plans.

One day in April Larissa asked Tom, "Why do we have to wait for May? We can honeymoon then, but let's get married now."

"That's fine with me," Tom said, "but what's the rush?"

"I think I'm pregnant."

"Well, let's plan to get married as soon as we can find a minister."

Arrangements were made for the following weekend. After a quiet ceremony, Tom and Larissa took a brief honeymoon at Stone Mountain, just outside Atlanta. "I promise you a bigger honeymoon next month," Tom told Larissa on their return.

"Who needs a bigger honeymoon? Are you as happy as I am?" Larissa asked her new husband.

Tom answered with a big kiss. "How's that for a reply?" he asked when they broke apart.

Several weeks later Larissa told Tom, "It looks as if the honeymoon will have to wait. This morning sickness would spoil our trip. Do you mind if we postpone our going away?"

"Who cares about the trip, honey? I just want you to feel better. We can go away any time."

Larissa felt miserable the whole nine months so there was no more talk about a honeymoon trip. But all the discomfort was forgotten that January when Thomas Desmond, Jr. was born.

"He's so beautiful. Look at those big dark eyes," Tom said to his wife. "Thank you for giving me such a gift."

Larissa, who had resigned from her job months before because she didn't feel well enough to go on working, was happy to be free so she could breastfeed Tommy.

When they began talking about the trip again, Larissa reminded Tom that they would have to take Tommy because she was still breastfeeding. "Would you rather wait until he's drinking from the bottle or cup?" she asked.

"No problem. We can take him. But we have to wait to the end of the school year."

They discussed the places they would like to go on their trip that May. "Wouldn't it be a crazy idea if we went to Longwood?" Tom asked Larissa. "It's a resort area, and we could rent a cottage on the lake."

"And you could visit Judy?" Larissa added.

"Would you mind?"

"Why should I? I'm secure in our marriage. Judy might like to see your son. I would like to meet her, too."

"You are something else," Tom said giving his wife a hug.

"Why don't you write to her and ask her if we could stop by?" Larissa suggested to Tom a few weeks before they were ready to leave. "Maybe she is married or maybe she just doesn't want to see us."

Tom wrote the letter that night and put it in his wallet planning on mailing it the next day when he had to go to the post office.

"Honeymoon, here we come," Tom sang as he packed the car one sunny day in May after school was out for summer vacation.

"A perfect day for a trip," Larissa observed when she belted Tommy into his car seat in the back seat of the car.

"I have a funny feeling we shouldn't be going," Larissa told Tom as they belted themselves into the front seat.

"Why?" Tom wondered. "Are you nervous about meeting Judy?"

"I guess. Never mind. It's bad luck to change plans."

PART II

"It doesn't look good," the first police officer on the scene told the State Trooper. "I don't think they knew what hit them." The police officer continued to try to revive Tom and Larissa and the driver who broadsided them ten miles from Longwood.

"Look! The baby is still alive." The officer worked on the baby while they waited for the ambulances from Longwood. No one was able to revive any of the adults, but the baby was still alive but badly injured.

After the ambulance left, the State Troopers searched the car for identification. Looking through Tom's wallet one officer found the letter Tom had not mailed. "There's an address on the envelope for someone in Longwood. Let's contact this person. Someone is going to have to care for the baby. Maybe this person is a relative."

I was shocked to see the Trooper at her door and even more shocked when I heard about the accident. After the letter was given to me and I read it, I asked the Trooper if he would be kind enough to take me to the hospital. When asked if I knew of any relatives, I replied, "I know Tom had no relatives and from what he said in the letter, Larissa had no relatives either. What will become of the baby?"

"The social services department will probably put him in a foster home and he'll probably be put up for adoption."

"Is there any chance I could take care of him?" I asked the officer.

"I don't know ma'am. You'd have to find out. Why would you want to take care of a Black baby anyway?"

"A baby is a baby," I replied. I didn't want to share with this stranger that I knew Tom and was almost married to him.

"What will become of the bodies of the baby's parents?" I continued.

"If there are no relatives I imagine the county would take care of the funeral. Why do you want to know?"

"I was just curious."

While the baby was recuperating, I visited every day. Meantime, I arranged for the two funerals. And she investigated the possibility of adopting the baby. I was finally allowed to become a foster mother.

"We are a little leery of interracial adoptions," I was told.

"A baby is a baby," I argued. But everyone turned a deaf ear regarding the adoption. "We are going to look for a Black family," the social services department insisted.

When the baby was well enough to leave the hospital, I brought Thomas Desmond, Jr. home.

"You're setting yourself up for a lot of problems," my mother warned. "I hope you know what you are doing, but your father and I will stand by you. You certainly are going to need all the support you can get."

Little did my parents realize that this baby might have been their grandchild. They never knew of my love for the baby's father.

"Who wouldn't love this baby?" I said. "He's such a darling."

"People are funny, Judy. A Black baby with a white mother, especially in our small town, will bring alot of remarks and even loss of friendship. I really am not optimistic."

My parents took care of the baby while I was in school during the day. When they took him out in the carriage I had bought they did get the strange looks they feared they would get. When word got around that I was caring for a Black baby, I noticed that people with whom I had been friendly no longer talked to me or treated me coldly. My parents were right. People are funny.

"What's wrong with people?" I asked my parents one night at dinner. "He's such a good baby. What does it matter what his skin color is?" My parents shrugged. It was then that I told them about Tom. Tears rolled down my cheeks as I remembered my last conversation with Tom.

My parents couldn't believe what they were hearing but as they had promised, they told me that they would not abandon me.

Tommy remained with me as a foster child. He grew into a bright little boy. Still no adoptive parents could be found. No word came from the social services department by the time Tommy was ready to begin school, so I enrolled him in the local elementary school.

I had continued to ask about adoption all along but now that Tommy was in school, I wanted to finalize an adoption and became more aggressive in my demands. I was delightfully surprised and thrilled when not long after that, I found out I could indeed apply for adoption.

"Persistence pays," I explained to everyone who asked how I did it.

Actually the authorities had been impressed with the care I had given Tommy and the love we felt for each other. Before long Tommy became Thomas Desmond Mann.

PART III

One day when Tommy's class had a field trip to the state police headquarters, Judy came along as chaperone. I saw a familiar face but couldn't place it.

"Pardon me for staring," I said, "but you look familiar. Where have I seen you before?"

"I was the Trooper who came to your house a few years ago to tell you about an automobile accident."

"Yes, now I remember. The baby who survived that accident is now my son."

"I am not surprised. I remember how concerned and compassionate you were. Have you had any problems raising him—I mean because of the difference in color?"

"Don't ask. At first, it was very hard. But I loved him and we have survived."

"You're a very courageous woman. May I ask, have you ever married?"

"No, I've been too busy teaching and raising my son."

"My name is Ed Roberts. I'm single. May I call you sometime? Your name is Judy Mann, isn't it?"

"You have a fantastic memory. Yes, you may call."

Ed and I began dating. We found out that we had many things in common. And Tommy and Ed hit it off, too. After a few months we began talking about marriage. I worried about having children because our children's skin would be white and Tommy might feel left out or resentful. Finally we decided to get married but decided not to have any children.

"Tommy will be my son after I adopt him. I feel he is my son already," Ed said. "How could I have been lucky enough to have found such a wonderful man?" I said snuggling up to Ed.

"Let's tell Tommy we're getting married. By the way we have to set a date."

"How about when school is out for the summer so we can take Tommy with us on our honeymoon?"

"Do you really want Tommy with us on our honeymoon?"

"Why not? We're family, aren't we?"

I sadly thought to myself, "Years ago Tommy was going with his parents on a honeymoon. Now he's finally going to take a honeymoon trip. I hope it has a happier ending than last time."

And it did. We toured several states after a small wedding in my parents' garden. We returned to a large five room apartment we had found before the wedding, glowing with happiness.

One day after school began in September Tommy came home and asked us when we were going to have a baby.

"We're not, honey," I explained. "You're all the family we want."

"I want a brother or sister. Why can't I have one?"

Ed and I tried to explain that there would be a difference in the baby's skin color and his skin color and that might cause problems.

"But your skin color is different than mine," Tommy argued. "And we get along just fine."

"How like your real father," I thought to myself. "He also said color doesn't matter."

"We'll think about it, Tommy," Ed said.

"Well think fast. I'm not getting younger," Tommy said.

After Tommy went out to play, we laughed at Tommy's statement, then talked seriously about having a baby.

When Tommy came in for dinner I told him, "Young man, we have decided to have a baby."

"Can I have a brother instead of a sister? Girls are no fun."

"Thanks alot." Judy faked displeasure.

Ed laughed. "That's Judy's son for you."

PART EIGHT

WHAT HAVE WE DONE?

Eight years ago as part of a unit on community helpers, I took my kindergarten class on a field trip to the local police station to learn about the work of policemen.

That evening my phone rang. Picking it up I heard the sweetest masculine voice ask, "Are you the Miss Cooper who brought the kindergarten class to the police station today?"

Warily I said that I was, and asked why he wanted to know.

"I heard one of the children call you Miss Cooper. I've been on the phone for an hour calling all the Coopers in the book trying to find you."

"Why?" I repeated.

"First, let me introduce myself. I am the officer who spoke to your class today. My name is Aaron Fox. I was taken by the kind way you treated the children and I want to meet you. I am single and I am not a pervert."

My ears perked up when he said he was single. I was single too, so when he suggested we meet at a local restaurant, I agreed.

"By the way, what is your first name?"

"Dulcie."

"Well, Miss Dulcie Cooper, see you tomorrow night."

When I hung up I realized I had just made a date with someone I didn't know. But I figured it was in a public place so it would be safe.

"Maybe this is Mr. Right," I said to myself. "There had been so many Mr. Wrongs in the past."

The next night I dressed carefully. Even though I was in my early thirties, I still had a slim figure. Looking through my closet I chose my navy blue dress with red collar, red cuffs, and multi-colored red belt. Then I took my navy blue shoes off the shoe rack. In my dresser I found a pair of navy blue stockings. After getting dressed, I combed my long blonde hair back away from my face and fastened a diamond hair clip in it. Then I applied eye shadow to highlight my light blue eyes. Admiring myself in the full-length mirror in my bathroom, I decided to wear my red coat and carry the red purse I had bought to go with it.

"Smashing," I thought to myself.

In the excitement I had forgotten what Aaron looked like, but I needn't have worried. As soon as I came through the door Aaron recognized me, came forward from the table he had reserved for us and escorted me back to the table. His rugged good looks, blonde hair, and smiling blue eyes took my breath away. I had to chuckle to myself when I saw he, too, was dressed in navy blue, a double breasted blazer and slacks, with a white turtleneck sweater.

Aaron noticed this, too. Simultaneously we said, "We could be twins," and laughed.

When we were seated, he squeezed my hand. "I'm so glad you came. I hope we will be friends."

Shivers ran down my spine. I had taken an instant liking to him, and couldn't believe I felt so good about someone I had just met.

Over dinner I learned that Aaron was also in his early thirties, never married, and had been a policeman ever since he graduated from college with a degree in police science. We compared our likes and dislikes and talked about everything we could think of. It was incredible how many things we had in common.

"We could almost be twins," I told Aaron. He smiled.

When Aaron walked me home, we held hands. He asked, "Do you feel as I do, that this is love at first sight?"

I was so overwhelmed with happiness I could only nod.

At my door I invited Aaron in. I ached to put my arms around him and kiss him fully. But Aaron refused to come in.

"This is happening so fast," he explained. "Let's wait to be sure."

I settled for a light kiss goodnight and a date for the following night.

The following night we went to the movies, the night after that to a concert, and the night after that we went bowling. Each night Aaron only gave me a light kiss goodnight. I was growing impatient to be in his arms.

"Let's stay home tomorrow night," I suggested when Aaron wanted to know if I had any ideas for the next night.

When Aaron arrived the next night I met him at the door in black and lace lounging pajamas. "Wow," was all he could say. Taking off his coat and putting it on the coat rack near the front door, he encircled my body with his powerful arms and kissed me deeply. Then he picked me up and gently put me down on my couch. I put my arms around him, hungrily returning his kisses. As he pulled me toward him with one arm, his other hand reached into my pajama bottom and massaged between my legs, slowly. I put my hand over his leading him to where I wanted to be touched. His massage became stronger, his kisses more insistent. Sparks flew through my body. He lay me down on the couch and tenderly entered my body. We reached the peak of excitement together. We lay locked together. It felt so good. We made love a second time.

"Stay for the night," I begged when Aaron realized it was getting late.

"Can't, honey. I have to be at work early tomorrow morning. Besides I don't have my uniform here."

I tried to arouse him.

"Now be a good girl and let me go." He gave me a playful spank on my behind.

I stiffened. "Don't you ever hit me again," I warned, tears beginning to course down my cheeks.

"What did I do? I was only joking."

I repeated, "Don't you ever hit me again." I was shaking.

"Tell me what's wrong." Aaron was shocked at my outcry. He led me over to the couch and made me sit down with him. "Why are you so upset?"

"When I was a little girl of about seven or eight, I had a big argument with my mother and called her a name I didn't even know the meaning of. I don't even remember what we argued about. But I ran out of the house and hid in the car in the garage, thinking no one could find me. I didn't see my dad come into the garage with a switch in his hand. He grabbed me out of the car and pulled me free. He bent me over and hit me with the switch I don't know how many times. Hearing my screams my mom came out of the house and made him stop.

"Apologize to your mother," he commanded.

Head bent low in shame, I mumbled, "I'm sorry."

"I can't hear you. Say it louder."

"I said it already," I said, shaking with pain and anger.

With his left hand he picked up my chin. With his right he delivered a stinging slap to my cheek.

"When I tell you to do something, you do it. Now say it louder."

Choking on my tears I managed to say it louder.

Dad took a painful grip on my arm and marched me back into the house and upstairs to my bedroom. "You stay here until I say you can come out. I'll hit you with the switch again if you disobey. And your mother won't stop me next time." He slammed the door.

"I fell on the bed and rolled over on my stomach crying hysterically. I lay there for hours in pain. No one came to see how I was."

"Didn't your mother come to check on you?" Aaron interrupted.

"No. I didn't know until some time later that the reason my dad was so upset was because my mom had just found out she had cancer, and she only had a short time to live. She died a few months later. Mom had wanted to come upstairs but she was too ill to walk the stairs.

"By the time I was let out of my room I had made up my mind I would never let anyone hit me again. I also made up my mind I'd never forgive my dad for what he did. My dad never hit me again or apologized for that brutal beating, so it was easy to stay angry at him. After my mom died, I went to live with my grandparents and didn't see too much of him anyway. He died in an automobile accident the following year. Now that I know why dad was upset, I have forgiven him, but I still will not let anyone hurt me.

"Living with my grandparents taught me to love again. I think I got my love for children from them. They took in foster children and I helped them. Though Grandpa was loving he was also strict, but he never hit me or any of the children they cared for. He made us work hard. He took away privileges. The worst punishment was what I called verbal spankings. If you did wrong, you got two earsful of yelling. Sad to say my grandparents are no longer alive."

Finally my story was over, and I leaned my head back on Aaron's shoulder.

"I'm sorry for what your dad did and for what I did," Aaron apologized. "On second thought, I am going to stay over. I can get up a bit earlier and get my uniform before I go to work."

"I'm so happy you'll stay. I love you. I need you."

That night we made love again but more than that, Aaron held me in his arms covering my face with kisses. I could feel the pain and anger of the past slip away.

"Let's get married," Aaron said the next evening. "I have a vacation in June and the school year is over. How would you like to go to Barbados for a honeymoon?"

I kissed him sweetly.

"I assume the answer is yes."

"Yes, oh yes."

We decided on a small church wedding. Neither one of us had any family, and we didn't want anything too elaborate anyway.

We made love again all night. We couldn't get enough of each other.

In April I realized I hadn't gotten my period. I went to the drug store and got a pregnancy test kit. Sure enough the result was positive. I met Aaron at the door that night crying.

"What's the matter, honey?"

"I'm pregnant."

"That's nothing to cry about. We'll get married now instead of June."

And that's what we did. On a cold, rainy Saturday that April we eloped to a nearby state and got married by a Justice of the Peace. We never did go to Barbados, though.

We spend the next seven months planning our future and planning for the baby. We were going to buy a house. I was going to stay home because we wanted more children. We refused the obstetrician's offer to tell us the gender of the baby after a sonogram was done. "We want to be surprised," I told him. But we were planning to have a boy, name him Aaron, Jr., and call him Ronnie so he wouldn't be confused with his dad.

Two weeks before the baby was due, Aaron was killed by a speeding motorist while he was directing traffic around an automobile accident. I was beside myself with grief and anger that Aaron was taken from me. If it hadn't been for the kind help of the minister of the church where we were supposed to get married and his darling wife, I don't know how I would have managed. They took care of the funeral arrangements and let me stay with them, tenderly caring for me until I went into labor, and then afterwards letting me and the baby stay with them until I was strong enough to go back to work. They even babysat for me so I wouldn't have to get a nanny when I returned to work. I shall always be grateful to them for their kindness and devotion.

I was still numb with shock when I went into labor. I had to have a cesarean because the baby was breech, so I was not awake when the baby was born. Through the haze when I awoke I heard the doctor say, "You have a beautiful baby girl."

"Are you sure? We were planning to have a boy."

The doctor looked at the baby again. "Yes, I'm sure. She's a girl and she's yours."

Tears poured down my cheeks when she was placed in my arms. She looked just like Aaron with her golden hair and big round blue eyes.

Later as we were snuggling in bed I realized we had not prepared a girl's name. I looked at the baby again thinking of names. I finally decided to name her Aarona and call her Rona. "That way your father will always be with us," I said to my daughter, who at the moment was trying to find my breast.

It was extremely painful going back to the apartment and going back to work. I ached for Aaron's kiss and strong arms. I needed him so.

But I had to make a living so I pushed myself every day to leave my baby and go to school.

That semester there was a three-day teachers' conference in an elegant hotel halfway across the state. I didn't want to go, but my minister and his wife urged me to go, telling me it would help me out of my depression. I went and there I met Zackery Thompson. He was a social studies teacher in a school not far from where my school was. He was forty, a bit older than I, a widower, with a young boy named Alex. With dark hair and piercing brown eyes, Zackery looked nothing like Aaron. He introduced himself at lunch on the first day, and we became acquainted.

His wife had died a year earlier from a stroke and he was having a hard time raising his son alone. I told him I was also single, a widow with a baby to raise alone.

We shared alot of time that weekend and decided to continue seeing each other when we got home.

I met Alex, a young man of nine. He was fun to be with and Zackery and I spent alot of time going to his school events and sports events.

"Where did he get his blonde curly hair from?" I asked Zackery one day.

"From his mother."

Zackery met Rona and fell in love with her cute ways.

Alex and Rona met. Well, Alex met Rona. He was fascinated with her, "even though she's a girl," he commented.

Zackery and I continued to see each other. Rona began to call Zackery daddy and began worshipping Alex who was not always thrilled having her tag alone with him and his friends.

Finally we decided to get married. Zackery needed a mother for his son, and I needed a father for my daughter. Ours was a quiet type of love. Zackery didn't sent flames through my body as Aaron did, but we needed each other.

I gave up my apartment and went to live in Zackery's house because it was larger and Rona would have her own room.

We got married quietly one June day after school was out for the summer.

For a honeymoon we went to Disney World. It wasn't as unromantic as it sounds. Every night after the children were asleep, Zackery and I would slip into the hot tub in the bathroom of our hotel room, massage each other all over with sweet smelling body oil, then kissing each other lightly on the lips at first, more insistent later, we got into bed where we made love until dawn, separating to put our pajamas on before the children woke up.

Zackery adopted Rona and I adopted Alex. Zackery and I discussed our philosophy about child raising. I made it clear I would not let Zackery spank our children. I told him what had happened to me, but he said that sometimes a spanking is necessary. I was surprised at his attitude because he was a teacher. When he said that sometimes in order to straighten a child out, you have to bend him over your knee, I pointed a finger at him warning him not to lay a hand on our children or I'd leave him.

Over the years Rona and Alex were sent to their room at times, had their allowance withheld at times, made to sit in the corner at times as punishment, but Zackery never hit the children, though at times he said to me when we were alone, "A good rump roast would do a better job of discipline." All in all the years were peaceful.

When Rona was seven and Alex a junior in high school, Zackery took a sabbatical to study to become a school administrator. He went away to college while I stayed home with the children so their schooling wouldn't be interrupted and I could continue teaching. By then Alex was taller than his dad and more muscular. He reminded me of Aaron in so many ways. With Zackery away he began helping me with the chores and babysitting Rona when I had to be away from the house. I fantasized he was Aaron.

One night after Alex and Rona went to bed, I lay down on the couch to watch television. I fell asleep and dreamt of Aaron. Half asleep I felt something on my thigh. Dreaming it was Aaron, I placed my hand over it and guided it between my legs where I wanted it as I had done with Aaron so many times. Next thing I knew something heavy was on top of me. Fully awake by then I saw it was Alex. "What are you doing?" I whispered loudly because I didn't want to wake up Rona.

"I love you. I have for a long time. Let me make love to you."

"Are you crazy? Get off me and go to bed and never do this again." I sat up to push him off me. He caught me as I arose and kissed me fully on the mouth. I tried to push him away but he was not about to be denied. He kissed me again. He pushed me back on the couch and began caressing me. God forgive me, but I responded, I couldn't resist. I think I was still dreaming of Aaron. When I realized what we were doing, I pushed Alex off the couch and told him I'd tell his father if he didn't go to bed immediately.

It was not easy trying to get to sleep that night. I was upset with myself for responding to Alex.

Alex did not get discouraged by what had happened that night. He tried arousing me many times during the next few weeks, and I kept pushing him away, threatening to tell his dad if he didn't stop.

Zackery returned from his sabbatical a changed person. He shouted at the children, especially Alex. He was especially rough on his son. He criticized Alex constantly, broke Alex's TV as punishment, took the car Alex had bought with his own money and sold it, also as punishment. Several times, I learned later, when I wasn't home he viciously beat Alex with a belt. He once wanted to spank Rona when I wasn't there, but Alex wouldn't let him. In return Zackery grabbed Alex and smashed his head against the wall several times, telling Alex he'd kill him next time he tried to stop him from disciplining Rona.

I didn't understand Zackery at all, but I tried to talk to him, to try to find out why he had changed. It was useless. He didn't seem to know what I was talking about.

Without telling me his father had beaten him, Alex turned to me for comfort, claiming he had broken off with a girlfriend. I sympathized with him and told him everything would be all right.

It wasn't long before I took to comforting Alex by holding him in my arms because he seemed so unhappy. He responded. We made love in his bed one day when there was no one at home. I was surprised how skillful he was. I was also surprised at myself for wanting him. It was exciting having a young man touch me, arouse me, make me tingle all over.

It was during this time Alex told me about the abusive ways of his father.

"Please don't say anything to dad. I'm afraid he'll kill me. I can take his abuse. I'll be out of the house before long." I felt sad that Alex would be graduating at the end of this school year and going away to college.

Zackery couldn't find a job as school administrator and I credited his continued unstable ways to his anxiety about not finding a job. The children bravely put up with his ranting and raving. I adjusted to this too as best as I could.

One day when Alex and I were again alone he told me he had an idea.

"I know dad has a gun. If I shoot him in the head when he's asleep it will look like suicide, and we'll be free of him."

As much as I had come to dislike Zackery, I thought it was a crazy idea and told Alex to forget it, the idea was just to bizarre.

One Saturday I had to go to the library to do some research for a project I wanted to do with my class. Alex was away on one of his infrequent jaunts with his friends. Rona was home alone with Zackery. I didn't plan to be away too long so I figured it would be all right to leave her with him.

Pulling into the driveway on my return I heard Rona screaming in her bedroom. Running to the house I opened the door and ran to her bedroom. There I saw Zackery sitting on the edge of Rona's bed. Rona was draped over his knee with her pants down. Zackery was bringing his belt down on Rona's behind again and again.

I ran over and pulled the belt out of his hand and pulled Rona off him. She clung to me sobbing that she hadn't done anything.

"Honest, mom, I just was reading a book on the porch when dad came up and dragged me up to my bed where he flung me over his knee, claiming I had broken the VCR. Honest, I didn't do anything."

"I believe you, honey. I don't know what's wrong with dad."

I calmed Rona down and got her to take a nap. Then I went downstairs where I found Zackery in the kitchen.

"Don't you ever hit Rona again," I raged at him.

"Don't you ever again interfere with how I discipline our—notice I said our—daughter. She broke the VCR and needed to know she did wrong."

I went into the living room and saw that there was nothing wrong with the VCR.

"What's wrong with you? There's nothing wrong with the VCR." I was furious.

"Maybe you need to feel my belt," he threatened.

"Don't you dare. I'll call the police so fast you wouldn't know what happened to you."

I tried to report this to our doctor asking him for advice, telling him Zackery needed some help because I thought there was something wrong.

The doctor just patted my hand.

"A father is entitled to discipline his children. You'll be laughed at if you report him. When I was a boy, spanking a naughty child was part of a father's duty. My dad spanked me and I grew up all right."

I was frustrated with him and stormed out of his office. Alex's idea of killing Zackery and making it look like suicide suddenly sounded appealing.

When I got home I waited for Alex to come home. I whispered to him so Rona, who was also home, wouldn't hear.

"Get your dad's gun and do what you said you'd do."

That night that's exactly what he did, but in the excitement he shot twice instead of only once. Then he put the gun in Zackery's hand and he called 911 sobbing, "Come quick. My dad shot himself. I think he's dead."

The police and the ambulance did some quickly. Zackery was indeed dead and the police did indeed think it was suicide. The body was taken away for an autopsy.

Rona was overcome with guilt, thinking she had caused her daddy to die. She never knew about Alex and me. We were very discreet. After we got Rona settled and she had fallen asleep in her bed, Alex and I retired to his bed where we congratulated ourselves on the perfect crime. Alex was so happy to be free of his father's tyranny. He was especially loving that night. He massaged my back from top to bottom making my body throb with desire. I put my arms around him, then massaged his firm young buttocks until he pulled me tight to his body and we made love. I left his room during the night and reluctantly returned to my bed so Rona would not know.

Rona went to school but Alex and I stayed home, playfully teasing each other, loving each other until it was time for Rona to come home. This went on for a few days.

A few days later there was a knock on the door. Opening it I saw two policemen and a woman who introduced herself as a social worker. Alex and I were arrested for murder. We protested but were told anything we said could be held against us so we shut up. The social worker roughly picked up Rona and ran to her car to take her to a foster home. If I live to be a hundred I'll never forget Rona screaming, "Mommy, don't let her take me away. What did I do? Mommy. Mommy." As the car pulled away I could hear her screaming, "Mom mee . . ."

Alex and I were taken to jail and each assigned our own attorney. Bail was denied. We are both in jail awaiting trial. I asked my attorney what made the authorities know it wasn't suicide.

If there had been only one bullet, you could have gotten away scot free. The fact that the autopsy showed there were two bullets made the authorities realize it wasn't suicide."

My attorney wasn't too happy representing me because of Alex and my affair. He added, "The autopsy showed you husband had Alzheimer's. You killed a sick man."

He wanted me to feel guilty about that.

Finally I knew why Zackery acted strangely but at the time I didn't care. All I cared about was my sweet Rona.

"What will become of Rona?"

"If you are found guilty and there is no family to take your daughter, she will be place for adoption."

I gasped. Neither Zackery, Aaron or I had anyone.

I spend my days in my cell feeling more and more guilty each day for all the pain I have caused my daughter and for not doing more for Zackery. I pace back and forth clutching Rona's picture to my breast and sobbing, "Rona, please forgive me. What have we done? What have we done?"

PART NINE

MY MOTHER IS ALSO
MY MOTHER-IN-LAW

Long before the sun came up on my wedding day last August, I heard my mother rattling around in the kitchen so I went downstairs to see if she was all right. Coming through the doorway I saw that she was eating breakfast. Seeing me she apologized, "I'm sorry if I woke you up, Fred. I am too excited to sleep. Want to join me?" Even though I wasn't fully awake yet, I said, "Sure, Mom." My mom was a new widow. She was nervous about my moving out after Rose and I came back from our honeymoon. She was afraid of being alone.

I had graduated from college in the northern part of the state in June and had been living with my mom until I moved into the small apartment Rose had found when she came to town in June. She, too, had graduated from college with me, and had come here rather than going back to her dad who lived in a nearby state. She wanted to get settled in and become acquainted with the area. We were going to begin teaching in the local school in September; Rose in a second grade, I in the social studies department of the high school.

Friends couldn't understand why I hadn't moved into the apartment with Rose as soon as she found it. We had decided when we first became serious in our sophomore year that we would not live together until we were married. Also, now that my mother was a new widow, she needed me for comfort and help in getting matters settled. I had no brothers or sisters so she had only one on whom she could rely.

"Don't be nervous about being alone," I soothed my mom as we were having a second cup of coffee. "Rose and I will be close by and we'll see each other often. And we're only a phone call away if you need us in between times."

Changing the subject, mom asked me if Rose's dad had arrived yet. He was a widower and since Rose, too, was an only child, she and her dad were very close. Rose's mom died when Rose was ten years old. Rose and my mom had met and become very fond of each other, but my mom had never met Rose's dad, and she was looking forward to meeting him.

"He arrived last night. He's staying at Rose's apartment."

"Where? The place is so small."

"He slept on the couch. He wanted to go to a motel but Rose wouldn't hear of it."

"My next door neighbor asked me why the wedding was going to be here rather than in Rose's hometown where her dad lives," my mom said wanting to make more conversation to prolong the time we were together.

"What did you tell her?"

"I told her it was easier for Rose's dad to come here than it was for me to go there."

"Why are people so nosy?"

"She was just being neighborly. Don't make anything of it."

"Fred, why don't you ask Rose and her dad to come here for lunch. We don't have to be at the hotel until the late afternoon. It would give us a good chance to become acquainted."

"Can't do that, Mom."

"Why not?"

"Because the bride and groom are not supposed to see each other on the day of the wedding before the ceremony.

"Silly custom," my mom said. "Oh well, there will be plenty of time to become acquainted. Rose told me that her dad will be staying at her apartment for a few days after the wedding because he wants to become familiar with the area. I'll invite him over for a meal then."

After that early breakfast, I urged mom to take a nap because there would be plenty of excitement later on. I left to take care of some last minute details.

The day's hours flew by and before we knew it my mom and I were on the way to the hotel where the ceremony and the reception would be held. We wanted to be there early before our guests arrive.

Rose and her dad must have had the same thought, because they, too, arrived early. When Rose caught a glimpse of me, she ducked into the room set aside for her and her maid of honor. Her dad thought Rose was rude, but my mom explained about the custom of the bride and groom not seeing each other on the day of the wedding before the ceremony. Rose's dad shared my mom's opinion that it was a silly custom.

"Now that that is over, I'd like to properly introduce the two of you to each other. Mom, I'd like you to meet Rose's dad, Bill. Bill, my mom, Edith."

They shook hands, but then hugged each other. "What the heck, we're going to be family," Bill explained when my mom was a little embarrassed.

I excused myself to look for my best man who had promised to come early so we could go over the details one last time. Bill and my mom were deep in conversation when I left them.

At five o'clock on the dot Rose was walking down the aisle on the arm of her proud dad. She was so beautiful it took my breath away. When the ceremony was over, we went to the room where we would have dinner and dance to a small band I had hired for the evening. After everyone was inside, Rose and I were introduced as husband and wife and dance the first dance. Then I danced with my mom while Rose danced with her dad before everyone else was invited to dance.

During dinner I noticed my mom and Rose's dad laughing and dancing very often.

"I'm so glad they're enjoying themselves," I whispered to Rose.

We left for Hawaii that night, a trip for which both Rose and I had saved from our wages from part-time jobs during college. When we returned, my mom told us about the lovely time she and Bill had had at the wedding and during the time he stayed in town before he left to go back to his home. She told us that they were going to be staying in touch by phone and letter. She seemed to have forgotten her sorrow, and I was relieved. I must admit I felt nervous about leaving her alone so soon after my dad's death.

The school year began the day after Labor Day. Rose got busy with her young children and I with my high school students, but we saw my mom regularly. She regaled us with the phone conversations and letters she had from Bill whenever we saw her.

Before long it was March. Easter was the following week and Rose's dad was coming to spend the holiday. He had spent Thanksgiving and Christmas with us.

One night that week Rose shocked me with the announcement that she was pregnant and the baby would be due in September.

"We were taking care," I gasped. "We wanted to wait before having a baby. What happened?"

Rose was almost in tears at my reply. "Aren't you happy? Why are you angry?"

"Oh honey," I answered realizing how upset Rose was. "I'm not angry. Of course, I am happy. I just didn't expect it yet." I took her in my arms and held her close. "I love you so much," I whispered in her ear.

"Do the folks know?" I asked when Rose seemed to have calmed down.

"Not yet. I think we should tell them after my dad gets here."

"Let's wait until we're having our Easter dinner. It will be a nice Easter surprise for them."

And surprised they were. And excited, too. My mom began knitting baby clothes. She wanted to know if she should make them in pink or blue, but we told her we didn't want to know until it was born. So she made everything in green and yellow. Rose's dad offered to furnish the baby's room when we found a bigger place. He offered to buy some of the other things we needed for a bigger apartment since we were living in a furnished apartment and nothing there belonged to us.

"That's much too generous," I told Bill.

"How many times does a person have a first grandchild?" he said. "Let me help."

"Dad, you're so sweet," Rose told her dad when I told Rose of her dad's offer.

As soon as school was over in June, Rose and I went apartment hunting. We couldn't believe our luck when we found a large two bedroom apartment a block from my mom's house. She was thrilled when we told her. "Now I'll be able to see my grandchild often." Addressing Rose, she continued, "If you want to go back to work, I'll be happy to take care of the baby full-time. It would be better than leaving the baby with a stranger."

"You're very sweet," Rose answered, "but for the time being I want to be a stay-at-home mom."

We didn't move in completely until early August. We needed time to buy everything. Rose's dad did furnish the extra room as the baby's room and did help us buy some of the other things. He refused my offer to repay him. "I'd be insulted if you did that," he said.

We celebrated our first anniversary in our new home. "Who would have believed we'd have all this last year at this time?" Rose said marveling at the new furniture and curtains. "Isn't it wonderful how things worked out?" she added.

"Yes, wonderful," I said, giving her a small kiss on her forehead. "Wouldn't it be cute if you go into labor on Labor Day?"

"That would be all right with me. I feel like a blimp. Being big in the summer is no fun."

"Did the doctor say anything about why you're so big?"

"No, he just scolded me, telling me I'm gaining too much weight."

"Well, hold on. September will soon be here."

Sure enough Rose went into labor on Labor Day. About 2AM that day Rose woke me up screaming. "My water broke. Get me to the hospital quick."

"Settle down, honey. The doctor said not to come to the hospital until the labor pains are ten minutes apart."

"Forget what the doctor said. If you don't get me to the hospital right away, I'll have the baby here."

Jumping out of bed, I quickly put on my clothes and helped Rose down to the car.

"Faster," she urged as we drove toward the hospital.

"I'm going as fast as I can, honey. We'll be there very soon."

"I don't think I'll make it," she shrieked. After she said that I pushed the car's speed even higher. "We're all going to get killed at this speed," I yelled at her.

I breathed a sigh of relief when we pulled up to the emergency room door. Two nurses whisked Rose away to the obstetrics department while I parked the car. After I entered the hospital an aide led me to the obstetrics department and helped me into a gown so I could go into the delivery room.

Opening the door of the delivery room I heard crying and saw the doctor coming toward me with an outstretched hand. "Congratulations," he said shaking my hand. "You're the father of twins—a boy and a girl. Go meet your family. They are in your wife's arms."

Confused and excited at the same time, I went toward my wife and babies laughing and crying at the same time. "I'm so sorry I yelled at you," she apologized when I got to her. "Nothing to apologize for," I said. "Isn't it wonderful?" Rose cooed. "Yes, wonderful," I answered.

"How come the doctor didn't tell us you were having twins?"

"He didn't know. He said that one was behind the other so he didn't hear two heartbeats."

"No wonder you were so big. What do we do now?"

"First, wipe your eyes. Then go out, find a phone, and call our folks. Then go out and buy another crib. We'll be home in a few days."

Putting her head on my shoulder, she asked me what should be name the babies. "How about naming the boy for my father and the girl for your mother?" I suggested. "That's lovely," she agreed.

When my mom came to visit later that day we introduced her to Charles and Helen. Tears came to her eyes. "That's so kind of you. I know Bill will be thrilled, too."

Rose's dad came the next day. He and mom seemed to be sharing a private joke.

"All right, you guys, what's up?" Rose asked when she couldn't stand their secrecy any longer.

"We wanted to wait until after we returned before telling you but we'll tell you now. You surprised us. Now it's our turn to surprise you. Bill and I are getting married. We're going to elope and take a little honeymoon trip before Bill moves here to live in my house. We won't be away as long so don't worry about not having anyone to help."

Rose and I looked at each other. "We thought you two were up to something," Rose finally said. We congratulated both of them and there were kisses and hugs all around.

"Mom, do you know what?" I asked my mother after we all broke apart from each other's kisses and hugs.

"What?"

"After the two of you are married, I will be able to say that my mother is also my mother-in-law."